How We Teach Jesus

How We Teach Jesus

A Fresh, Practical Look at Christian Education in the Church

Bill Thomas

CSS Publishing Company, Inc
Lima, Ohio

HOW WE TEACH JESUS

FIRST EDITION
Copyright © 2023
by CSS Publishing Co., Inc.

Library of Congress Cataloging-in-Publication Data

Names: Thomas, Bill (Christian Educator), author.
Title: How we teach Jesus : a fresh look at Christian education in the church / Bill Thomas.
Description: First edition. | Lima, Ohio : CSS Publishing Company, Inc., [2022]
Identifiers: LCCN 2022054965 (print) | LCCN 2022054966 (ebook) | ISBN 9780788030680 | ISBN 9780788030697 (ebook)
Subjects: LCSH: Jesus Christ--Person and offices--Study and teaching. | Christian education.
Classification: LCC BT203 .T49 2022 (print) | LCC BT203 (ebook) | DDC 232--dc23/eng/20230120
LC record available at https://lccn.loc.gov/2022054965
LC ebook record available at https://lccn.loc.gov/2022054966

For more information about CSS Publishing Company resources, visit our website at www.csspub.com, email us at csr@csspub.com, or call (800) 241-4056.

e-book:
ISBN-13: 978-0-7880-3069-7
ISBN-10: 0-7880-3069-8

ISBN-13: 978-0-7880-3068-0
ISBN-10: 0-7880-3068-X

This book is dedicated to Judah Allyn Gilbert.
May you always want to learn more about Jesus.

Acknowledgments

I want to thank the following people for their help in this project:

David Runk, Karyl Corson and the entire team at CSS Publishing who do a great job of getting quality, Christian material to many different churches.

Dottie Bodewitz, who proofread the initial manuscript and helped get it ready.

Dave Smith, Dr. Anne Menear, Dr. Scott Womble and Dr. Minta Hardman, who read the manuscript and shared insights and ideas.

My Christian Education students, especially Sarah, Malachi, Stevie, Josh, and Brendan, who were the first to hear this material presented in class.

Contents

Introduction

Isaac Watts said, "Instructors should not only be skillful in those sciences which they teach, but have skill in the method of teaching, and patience in the practice."[1] This is true in many disciplines, but none more important than in Christian education. Over the years, the way churches approach Christian Education has changed dramatically. We've gone from age specific Sunday school classes, each equipped with a flannel graph and appropriate characters, to age-appropriately equipped, technologically advanced classes, many using smart boards and projectors.

The way we do Christian Education has changed over the years. There was a time when churches found a volunteer to be the Sunday school Superintendent and a different volunteer to be the Vacation Bible School coordinator. In those days, Christian Education was divided into departments that were led by a volunteer.

In the 1980s and 1990s, the approach changed. Christian Education was funneled through one staff person who had oversight over all aspects of it. The position of Christian Education minister was regularly found on many church staffs and he or she would oversee all the components of Christian Education that used to be under volunteer leadership.

Currently, in many churches, Christian Education is no longer a specific ministry. Instead, the principles and oversight of Christian Education are found in specific ministries. Children's ministers, student minsters, discipleship ministers and a host of others all utilize and manage how Christians today are taught and equipped.

1   Isaac Watts, "Inspirational Learning and Training Quotes," *TIS Quotes.*
    Link: https://techinspiringstories.com/quote-topics/trainer-quotes/

As the times change and the people we work with change, many of our principles and values do not. However, our methods and approaches must change. How do we teach people about Jesus and the Bible? How do people best learn? What do we do with our Sunday school classes? How do we train our teachers? How do we recruit and manage volunteers? How do we motivate those volunteers when there are tough times? How important is vetting and background checks? What policies need to be written and distributed among your volunteer staff? These questions and a host of others must be addressed by ministers and Christian teachers if we are to continue to teach, motivate and inspire people to be like Jesus. It's my prayer that this book will help.

Chapter 1

The Purpose of
Christian Education

"The big message of the Bible is God's plan to populate his new kingdom. Everything else is secondary." Max Lucado made this observation in his book *Max on Life: Answers and Insights to Your Most Important Questions*.[2] This is an accurate assessment of the process of Christian Education. Once a person enters a relationship with Jesus Christ, that person then embarks on a journey of learning and discovering what God has in store for him. Christian Education is the label we've often used to describe the process of learning and growing in the Lord Jesus Christ.

Biblical Imperative to Grow

Growing spiritually isn't optional for the Christian. Either you are growing, or you are regressing. There is no staying the same. The Bible makes it clear that it is God's intention for his people to grow. Consider the following…

Hebrews 6:1-3

Therefore let us move beyond the elementary teachings about Christ and be taken forward to maturity, not laying again the foundation of repentance from acts that lead to death, and of faith in God, instruction about cleansing rites, the laying on of hands, the resurrection of the dead, and eternal judgment. And God permitting, we will do so.

Luke 8:14-15

The seed that fell among thorns stands for those who hear, but as they go on their way they are choked by life's worries, riches and pleasures, and they do not mature. But the seed on good soil

2   Max Lucado; *Max on Life: Answers and Insights to Your Most Important Questions*, Thomas Nelson, Nashville, TN, 2010, p. 93

stands for those with a noble and good heart, who hear the word, retain it, and by persevering produce a crop.

Colossians 1:9-10

For this reason, since the day we heard about you, we have not stopped praying for you. We continually ask God to fill you with the knowledge of his will through all the wisdom and understanding that the Spirit gives, so that you may live a life worthy of the Lord and please him in every way: bearing fruit in every good work, growing in the knowledge of God.

Psalm 92:12-14

The righteous will flourish like a palm tree, they will grow like a cedar of Lebanon; planted in the house of the Lord, they will flourish in the courts of our God. They will still bear fruit in old age; they will stay fresh and green.

Growing in knowledge and understanding of Jesus Christ, the Bible and how to walk by faith is the life-long challenge of all who wear the name "Christian." It is also the responsibility of those of us, who are called to lead and teach, to facilitate and enable growth and create the environment best suited for learning. It is a challenging and serious task.

James 3:1

Not many of you should become teachers, my fellow believers, because you know that we who teach will be judged more strictly.

It is a sobering challenge, but it is one that can be immensely rewarding.

Howard Hendricks once wrote, "Every disciple needs three types of relationships in his life. He needs a 'Paul' who can mentor him and challenge him. He needs a 'Barnabas' who can come alongside and encourage him. And he needs a 'Timothy,' someone that he can pour his life into."[3]

That's the goal of what we do. Let's begin by looking at why it matters.

---

3   Howard G. Hendricks, "Howard G. Hendricks Quotes and Sayings," *Inspiring Quotes. us*, https://www.inspiringquotes.us/author/7943-howard-g-hendricks

Five Purposes of Christian Education

As we examine the broad topic called *Christian Education*, it doesn't take long to see that it is a multi-facet discipline that meets several different purposes in the church, the home, and in the life of a Christian. To begin, we need a uniform definition of Christian Education. The question "What is Christian Education and why is it important?" has been answered in different ways by lots of people over the years. For our purposes, I think the best definition is...

Christian Education — the process by which an individual can become more like Jesus and grow closer in a walk with him.

Using that definition as a foundation, we can springboard into the five different components or purposes of Christian Education.

Purpose #1

Introduce People to Jesus

The first of these is our primary challenge as Christians. Christian Education is the means by which we introduce others to Jesus Christ and what it means to follow him.

Glen Schultz, in his 1998 book *Kingdom Education: God's Plan for Educating Future Generations*, wrote, "the reality of the preeminence of Christ must be woven throughout every fiber of true education."[4]

The first purpose of Christian Education is to introduce others to Jesus Christ. That seems obvious, but I think many times it gets lost in the plethora of objectives, lessons and aims.

In John 3 we find Nicodemus, one of the leading teachers of the Jews, coming to ask questions of and learn from Jesus. The reason is evident. He wanted to know who he was and why he came. We don't hear much about Nicodemus again until he defends Jesus as recorded in John 7:50 and again in John 19:39 as he brings a mixture of myrrh and aloes for Jesus' body.

---

4   Glen Schultz, *Kingdom Education: God's Plan for Educating Future Generations*, Lifeway Publications, Nashville, TN, 1998, p. 30

It seems clear that the learning that took place on that night recorded in John 3 led to his introduction and acceptance of Jesus.

It isn't hard to find scriptural support for Christian teaching leading to Jesus.

Matthew 28:18-20

Then Jesus came to them and said, "All authority in heaven and on earth has been given to me. Therefore, go and make disciples of all nations, baptizing them in the name of the Father and of the Son and of the Holy Spirit, and teaching them to obey everything I have commanded you. And surely, I am with you always, to the very end of the age."

Romans 10:16-17

But not all the Israelites accepted the good news. For Isaiah says, "Lord, who has believed our message?" Consequently, faith comes from hearing the message, and the message is heard through the word about Christ.

Psalm 32:8

I will instruct you and teach you in the way you should go; I will counsel you with my loving eye on you.

Colossians 2:2-3

My goal is that they may be encouraged in heart and united in love, so that they may have the full riches of complete understanding, in order that they may know the mystery of God, namely, Christ, in whom are hidden all the treasures of wisdom and knowledge.

As administrators of Christian Education, it's imperative that we keep the focus on this purpose. Ideally, in our churches, we emphasize and develop a culture in which Christian Education begins and is centered in the home.

Larry Fowler of Focus on the Family writes, "For parents of young children, the journey of raising Christ followers starts with the task of instilling respect for God and his authority."[5]

Assisting parents in the journey of raising Christ followers is a big part of what we do. Beginning with our nursery programs, we can provide materials (coloring pages, story books, age-appropriate toys) that introduce Jesus and the Bible stories. Making these available to parents is important as we create a culture of life-long learners and followers of Jesus.

The tragic reality is, though, that not all the people that enter our churches come from Godly households. Many times, we are beginning from scratch with children and adults.

Our volunteer staff matters. All the volunteers in your ministry must understand that the primary objective they have, as they serve, is to introduce people to Jesus.

Your kindergarten teacher in Sunday school or Vacation Bible School is not just a kindergarten teacher. He or she is one of the first people ever to speak to a group of children about Jesus and the wonderful stories in the Bible.

We sometimes take it for granted, but for some children (those whose parents don't do much Christian teaching in the home), the early Sunday school or VBS classes are where they meet and encounter God, Moses, Noah, Abraham, David and Jesus.

You may have sung "Jesus Loves Me" a million times, but there was the *first* time. Someone taught it to you and sang it with you the first time. That "someone" may not have thought much about it, but what he or she was doing was introducing you and your peers to Jesus.

Your student ministry volunteer may be the first adult a young person has ever met that openly talks about following Jesus and putting him first. That volunteer is the first genuine "Christ-follower" that kid has ever met and is showing that student Jesus without ever realizing it.

5   Larry Fowler, "Introducing Your Child to God" *Focus on the Family*, 2009, www.focusonthefamily.com/parenting/spiritual-growth-for-kids/salvation-leading-your-child-to-Jesus/introducing-your-child-to-god

We must instill in our own hearts and the hearts of our ministry volunteers that every time we meet, we are introducing our people to Jesus.

Purpose #2

Discipling

The second purpose of Christian Education aligns closely with the first one. Once we've introduced people to Jesus, the challenge becomes helping, challenging and motivating them to walk with him.

Alexander Campbell, in *The Millennial Harbinger* in 1837, explains the important connection between Christian Education and growing in Jesus. He wrote, "A portion of the Lord's Day cannot be more profitably occupied than in teaching children to read or commit to memory the sacred scriptures, and in inculcating upon them the important principles of Christianity."[6]

Lawrence O. Richards writes, "The life we are given in Christ is God's own life. As that life grows in us, we become more and more like him."[7]

Seeing those under our influence become more like Jesus is one of the most rewarding aspects of Christian Education. The Bible makes it clear that growing in knowledge and understanding is crucial for living more as Jesus did.

Ephesians 4:16

From him the whole body, joined and held together by every supporting ligament, grows and builds itself up in love, as each part does its work.

6   Alexander Campbell, *The Millennial Harbinger* in Eleanor Daniel, *Leaven* 16, Issue 1, "Christian Education in the Stone-Campbell Movement" (Pepperdine University, January 2008), 5.

7   Lawrence O. Richards, *Christian Education: Seeking to Become Like Jesus Christ* (Zondervan: Grand Rapids, MI, 1975), 20.

2 Timothy 2:2

And the things you have heard me say in the presence of many witnesses entrust to reliable people who will also be qualified to teach others.

John 8:31-32

To the Jews who had believed him, Jesus said, "If you hold to my teaching, you are really my disciples. Then you will know the truth, and the truth will set you free."

Proverbs 27:17

As iron sharpens iron, so one person sharpens another.

Christian Education leaders should refuse to accept that it's enough that people just know Jesus as Savior without growing in him and becoming more like him. The teaching and environment we help create can foster a continual hunger for more of God's word and understanding.

This commitment to growth and discipleship is seen in different specific areas.

What curriculum do we choose? This is an important and practical question that everyone who's ever been entrusted with some component of Christian Education has had to face. We'll address this more specifically later, but the critical question as it related to the purpose is does this curriculum aid in the student's growth and having a closer walk with Jesus?

What kind of classes do we have? Are they organized by age or by interest? This is another of those routine questions with which ministry leaders grapple. Again, more on this later, but for now, does the structure we employ aid in or hinder the student's understanding and maturing?

How do we balance having fun and learning? For children's ministers and student ministers, this is a constant question. We want our groups to be engaging and appealing, but we aren't content that they be *only* fun and games. What is the balance and how do I achieve it? We'll examine this more specifically in a while, but for now, the environment needs to nurture growth.

In addition to this discussion, another significant component emerges. Does my ministry allow for or promote mentoring? This is a critical aspect of discipleship. What is mentoring? The coming alongside of another Christian to encourage, challenge and inspire him/her to be more like Jesus. Paul wrote to Titus about how important mentors can be.

Titus 2:1-5

You, however, must teach what is appropriate to sound doctrine. Teach the older men to be temperate, worthy of respect, self-controlled, and sound in faith, in love and in endurance. Likewise, teach the older women to be reverent in the way they live, not to be slanderers or addicted to much wine, but to teach what is good. Then they can urge the younger women to love their husbands and children, to be self-controlled and pure, to be busy at home, to be kind, and to be subject to their husbands, so that no one will malign the word of God.

Solomon knew the benefit good mentors could provide. He wrote...

Proverbs 13:20

Walk with the wise and become wise, for a companion of fools suffers harm.

Peter, too, writes of the value of mentoring.

1 Peter 5:1-5

To the elders among you, I appeal as a fellow elder and a witness of Christ's sufferings who also will share in the glory to be revealed: Be shepherds of God's flock that is under your care, watching over them — not because you must, but because you are willing, as God wants you to be; not pursuing dishonest gain, but eager to serve; not lording it over those entrusted to you, but being examples to the flock. And when the chief shepherd appears, you will receive the crown of glory that will never fade away. In the same way, you who are younger, submit your-

selves to your elders. All of you, clothe yourselves with humility toward one another, because, "God opposes the proud but shows favor to the humble."

In our culture today, we can't overstate the importance of people having others walk with them as they try to walk more like Jesus.

John Maxwell said, "The best way a mentor can prepare another leader is to expose him or her to other great people."[8] May that always be a part of what we do as we teach and instruct others.

Purpose #3

Equip for Service

A third purpose of Christian Education is to prepare others for profitable service in God's kingdom. We are not just pushing knowledge for the sake of knowing something. The thrust behind knowing something is to be able to **do** something with what you know. The Bible talks about this in terms of equipping people for service.

Ephesians 4:11-12

So, Christ himself gave the apostles, the prophets, the evangelists, the pastors and teachers, to equip his people for works of service, so that the body of Christ may be built up.

2 Timothy 3:16-17

All Scripture is God-breathed and is useful for teaching, rebuking, correcting and training in righteousness, so that the servant of God may be thoroughly equipped for every good work.

Hebrews 13:20-21

Now may the God of peace, who through the blood of the eternal covenant brought back from the dead our Lord Jesus, that great shepherd of the sheep, equip you with everything good for doing

---

8   John C. Maxwell, "John C. Maxwell Sayings and Quotes," *Wise Old Sayings*.
Link: https://www.wiseoldsayings.com/authors/john-c.-maxwell-quotes/

his will, and may he work in us what is pleasing to him, through Jesus Christ, to whom be glory for ever and ever. Amen.

Equipping people, both young and old, is an important facet of our Christian Education program. Our teaching needs to have a practical outlet. This can be seen in a variety of ways.

First, we must merge information and application.

We don't merely teach about loving others, we equip believers to love and give them opportunities to show it. We spend time explaining and demonstrating what the Bible says. For example, Mark 12:30-31 says, "Love the Lord your God with all your heart and with all your soul and with all your mind and with all your strength.' The second is this: 'Love your neighbor as yourself.' There is no commandment greater than these."

There is a lot to unpack in those verses and quality teaching compels us to do a good job on it. However, explanation is not enough. There ought to be application of it, too. Perhaps after teaching on this text, a service project can be planned. Maybe the junior high group can go rake leaves and clean the yards of senior saints in your church. Perhaps your small group can discuss this passage and then create a plan that will help single moms in your community. Your men's group could study this passage and then create a ministry to assist the disabled in your church.

Putting flesh on what we learn allows us to take Jesus to those who need to see him and experience his love. Information should lead to application.

Second, information must foster motivation.

It isn't enough to learn things for "learning's sake." When our students see and understand Jesus in ways they haven't before, it ought to create a hunger or a thirst for more. Once our students have tasted of the wonders of Christ and his love, it ought to launch an insatiable quest for more.

Kayt Sukel, in a business blog called *Big Think* wrote, "A few years ago, Lay's Potato Chips threw down the gauntlet in a new advertising campaign: 'Bet you can't eat just one!' It was a clever slogan — and had a clever commercial to match.

But I think the line resonated so much because it's true. It's quite difficult to eat just one chip."[9]

That's our goal in something far more important than chips. When the people we work with get a little of what Jesus is like, they shouldn't stop wanting more.

Finally, information should strengthen confidence and competence.

When we teach, we are building up those who hear us. We're allowing them to develop the gifts and talents God gave them and become more confident in using them. For example, when we teach about the person and work of Jesus, we're giving our students the information they need to be able to explain who Jesus is. They not only know who he is to them, but they have an awareness of who he is in the Bible and what he did. If we simply taught that, we'd be imparting knowledge. Not a bad thing, but less than what we might do. To go to the next level and meet this purpose, we allow our students a chance to internalize and perhaps even vocalize what it means to them. Either in discussion or in a small group, we allow them a chance to talk and make what we've taught their own.

People tend to be more confident when they've practiced. That's clear in sports, music and theater. The more a person practices, the more the action becomes natural. Why would that be any different when we're talking about spiritual things?

Max Lucado has called it "practicing the presence of God."[10] It involves yielding all my thoughts to the control of the Holy Spirit. It's something that I have to consciously choose to do. In other words, I have to practice it. The more I do that, the easier it becomes to do.

We should teach in such a way that our people learn and can put into practice what we're teaching.

9   Kayt Sukel, "The Science of 'Bet You Can't Eat Just One,'" *Big Think* (April 2013). bigthink.com/world-in-mind/bet-you-can't-eat-just-one

10   Max Lucado, "Practicing the Presence of God," Link: https://maxlucado.com/listen/practicing-the-presence-of-god/

Equipping for service is an integral part of Christian Education and needs to be an intentional part of our planning.

Purpose #4

Train for Righteousness

A fourth purpose of Christian Education is to train people for living a righteous life. As Peter writes, quoting Leviticus, in 1 Peter 1:16, "Be holy because I am holy." Christians are called to live a holy life and be more Christlike. That comes through being taught or trained to live that way. The Bible makes that clear.

1 Timothy 4:7-8

Have nothing to do with godless myths and old wives' tales; rather, train yourself to be godly. For physical training is of some value, but godliness has value for all things, holding promise for both the present life and the life to come.

Hebrews 5:11-14

We have much to say about this, but it is hard to make it clear to you because you no longer try to understand. In fact, though by this time you ought to be teachers, you need someone to teach you the elementary truths of God's word all over again. You need milk, not solid food! Anyone who lives on milk, being still an infant, is not acquainted with the teaching about righteousness. But solid food is for the mature, who by constant use have trained themselves to distinguish good from evil.

Proverbs 4:1-5

Listen, my sons, to a father's instruction; pay attention and gain understanding. I give you sound learning, so do not forsake my teaching. For I too was a son to my father, still tender and cherished by my mother. Then he taught me, and he said to me, "Take hold of my words with all your heart; keep my commands, and you will live. Get wisdom, get understanding; do not forget my words or turn away from them."

These passages demonstrate that our teaching is to take root in people and produce a righteousness which comes through faith. As we've noted earlier, it isn't enough to teach for knowledge's sake alone.

Richards writes, "We need to focus our educational efforts on understanding and using the church, the Body of Christ, as a culture within which persons who receive the gift of God's life, are to be involved, and through this involvement, be socialized into all it means to become like him."[11]

What does it look like to emphasize training for righteousness? There are a few factors that must be considered as we attempt to go deeper into the lives and hearts of our students.

First, we have to recognize that we live in a culture that runs counter to living as Jesus did. It doesn't require much research to discover that people today are moving, sometimes at an accelerated pace, away from the life that God desires his people to live. The people we engage with at our small group, Sunday school class or youth group are dealing with a culture that has become increasingly relativistic and selfish.

We are urging them to live lives differently than those around them. That sounds nice to say and it's easy to write, but what's much tougher is doing it. Are our lessons and discussions full of niceties and Christian-ese, or are we giving them something weighty and real that can help them live as light in a world that grows increasingly darker?

Second, we must commit to the principle that teaching is about life change. Bruce Wilkinson wrote in his book *The Seven Laws of the Learner: How to Teach Almost Anything to Practically Anyone*, "We get so tied up in our content that we forget the purpose of content is life change."[12]

Changing hearts and equipping our people to live for Jesus must be our passion. In our current culture, we can't settle for educated Christians who don't live any differently than those around them. Life change has to be a part of the DNA

11 Richards, Lawrence O. , *Christian Education: Seeking to Become Like Jesus Christ* (Zondervan: Grand Rapids, MI, 1975), 78.

12 Bruce Wilkinson, *Laws of the Learner: How to Teach Almost Anything to Practically Anyone* (Multnomah: NY, 1992), 139.

of all that we do in the church. Whether it be in worship, the classroom, the small group, the children's worship center, or the student activity center, if we are not driven by life change, we will produce ineffective and shallow followers of Jesus.

Finally, we have to be committed to a righteous life, ourselves, as we teach and instruct others. Paul noted this when he wrote in 1 Corinthians 9:27, "No, I strike a blow to my body and make it my slave so that after I have preached to others, I myself will not be disqualified for the prize."

Richards notes the importance of modeling when he says, "learning the Christian faith should be very much like learning speech or manners." In his view, it is not done in artificial situations, but in real ones. It isn't so much taught as it is caught. [13]

Righteous living matters. We can't teach and model that which we don't live. Teaching that is not accompanied by living it out is empty. It's important for us to see part of our role as teachers is equipping people to live for Jesus.

Purpose #5

Develop Confidence for Witnessing

The final aspect of the purpose of Christian Education is to aid our students in developing confidence to share their faith with other people. Richards writes, "It is important to recognize parallels between educational and evangelization ministries of the church." He continues to note that in each case the Word of God is involved, a faith response is desired, and, in each case, response is facilitated by relationship.[14]

Part of what we do as Christian educators is provide our students a framework from which to share their story. Our instruction can build confidence and comfort for talking to others about Jesus. The Bible speaks directly to that challenge.

---

13 Richards, *Christian Education: Foundations for the Future*, 82.

14 Richards, *Ibid*, pp. 51-52

1 Peter 3:15-16

But in your hearts revere Christ as Lord. Always be prepared to give an answer to everyone who asks you to give the reason for the hope that you have. But do this with gentleness and respect, keeping a clear conscience, so that those who speak maliciously against your good behavior in Christ may be ashamed of their slander.

Ephesians 6:15

and with your feet fitted with the readiness that comes from the gospel of peace.

1 Peter 1:13

Therefore, with minds that are alert and fully sober, set your hope on the grace to be brought to you when Jesus Christ is revealed at his coming.

1 John 2:28

And now, dear children, continue in him, so that when he appears, we may be confident and unashamed before him at his coming.

In our classes, small groups, kids' clubs, student ministries and adult Bible studies we are strengthening people in their resolve, boldness and skill as they share with others.

As we do so, there are a few things we need to keep in mind.

First, our instruction must convey the truth that it is our responsibility to share with others. We don't get to choose whether we want to do it. Paul writes in 2 Corinthians 5:18-20 these words.

All this is from God, who reconciled us to himself through Christ and gave us the ministry of reconciliation: that God was reconciling the world to himself in Christ, not counting people's sins against them. And he has committed to us the message of reconciliation. We are therefore Christ's ambassadors, as though God were making his appeal through us. We implore you on Christ's behalf: Be reconciled to God.

Jesus has called all his followers to become his ambassadors. The challenge to share the good news is for all Christians. It is part of the purpose of educating people in Christ that we acknowledge, challenge and develop the skills needed for them to accomplish it.

It's important, too, to note that there are different ways in which we teach people to do that. Our students need to be able to relate who Jesus is and what he means to them. Part of what we do is to help them develop this skill. We also recognize that witnessing with words isn't the only way to share Jesus. In fact, it might, in some cases, not be the best way. We also must implore those with whom we share that their lives reflect their walk with Jesus.

St. Francis of Assisi wrote in his Rule of 1221, Chapter XII on how the Franciscans should practice their preaching. In it he said, "No brother should preach contrary to the form and regulations of the holy Church nor unless he has been permitted by his minister... All the friars ...should preach by their deeds."[15]

James, the half-brother of Jesus, writes in James 2:18, "Show me your faith without deeds, and I will show you my faith by my deeds."

Helping others gain confidence and experience in witnessing is a vital component of a healthy, vibrant Christian Education approach.

Summary

Christian Education is an indispensable part of what we do in the church. It permeates nearly every ministry and has ramifications across nearly everything we do for Jesus. Before we progress into more specific components of it, let's review again the five purposes.

1. Introduce people to Jesus
2. Discipling
3. Equip for service
4. Train for righteousness

---

15 Glen Stanton, "Fact Checker: Misquoting St. Francis of Assisi," *The Gospel Coalition*, July 10, 2012, www.thegospelcoalition.org/article/factchecker-misquoting-francis-of-assisi/

5. Develop confidence for witnessing

These five components need to be an integral part of all we do as Christian teachers and leaders.

Questions for Reflection

1. The first part of this chapter discusses the imperative to grow. How much intentional thought and planning should be given to growth? Discuss that growth is more than just increasing numbers.

2. Consider all the Christian education you've received over the years. How many of your teachers were aware that they were introducing Jesus to you and the others in your class? Think back to who it was that told you about Jesus. Is there a connection between that moment and "Christian education?" Why or why not?

3. What hinders discipleship in the Christian education programs you've seen and known? How do we overcome those obstacles and do a better job of discipling?

4. What prevents equipping for service in the programs you've seen? How important is it? Why?

5. Do churches promote living a righteous life enough? What can we do to "do better?"

6. Why do you think many people are hesitant to share their faith? What is about sharing that is so scary? How can we aid them in overcoming it?

Chapter 2

Planning and Evaluation

As we scan human history, there seems to be a common thread that unites all of man's greatest achievements. Whether it be advances in medicine, architecture, technology or tools, there is a marvelous working together of God' revelation and human hard work. All great human endeavors have included a God-factor and a leadership factor. Success in whatever man has attempted has come about largely through the process called trial and error. What has fueled humanity's progress has been the adage, "if at first you don't succeed, try, try again," combined with the old teaching, "learn from your mistakes." It's the dance preparation does with evaluation. What's true in the course of human history, is true in the classroom or with the student ministry. Planning and evaluation matter.

Planning or Preparation

"A prepared teacher makes his classes fresh, vital and interesting. In return, his students are productive."[16] Planning and evaluating are vital components of any successful endeavor. Legendary basketball coach John Wooden once said, "Failing to prepare is preparing to fail."[17]

Lack of preparation can be disastrous. A British Arctic expedition set sail in 1845 to chart the Northwest Passage around the Canadian Arctic to the Pacific Ocean. The expedition was led by Captain Sir John Franklin. He had two ships with him and 138 men. Surprisingly, he packed a 1,200-volume library, a hand-organ, china place settings for officers and men, cutglass wine goblets and sterling silver flatware for a journey

---

16 Larry Richards and Lin Johnson, *Christian Education: Foundations for the Future,* ed, Robert E. Clark, Moody Press, Chicago, (1991), p. 171.

17 Jason Selk, "Failing To Prepare Is Preparing To Fail: How To Never Lose Again," *Forbes Magazine,* March 21, 2018, https://www.forbes.com/sites/jasonselk/2018/03/21/failing-to-prepare-is-preparing-to-fail-how-to-never-lose-again/#6d5b2f912b5e

through one of the earth's most hostile environments. He did not prepare for the extreme weather or climate. Neither of the two ships and none of the 138 men aboard returned.[18]

Biblical Imperative to Plan

While it may not be life-threatening, preparation makes a difference. When we talk about planning, we need to first identify what it isn't. The preparation and planning we're discussing here is not determining an outcome and a life-course and expecting God to deliver. It's not thinking we are in charge or the captains of our own destiny.

James writes against the foolishness of that when he says, "Now listen, you who say, 'Today or tomorrow we will go to this or that city, spend a year there, carry on business and make money. Why, you do not even know what will happen tomorrow. What is your life? You are a mist that appears for a little while and then vanishes." (James 4:13-14)

Planning in the context of teaching should not be misunderstood to mean we take the place of God and solely determine outcomes. It is the conviction that I must do all I can to put myself in a place where God can use me to the fullest. God expects his people to be wise in how they live and in what they do. Consider…

Luke 14:28

Suppose one of you wants to build a tower. Won't you first sit down and estimate the cost to see if you have enough money to complete it?

Proverbs 16:3

Commit to the Lord whatever you do, and he will establish your plans.

Proverbs 24:27

Put your outdoor work in order and get your fields ready; after that, build your house.

18 Annie Dillard, *Teaching a Stone to Talk*, Harper Collins, New York, (1988), p. 30.

Isaiah 32:8

But the noble make noble plans, and by noble deeds they stand.

Matthew 6:33

But seek first his kingdom and his righteousness, and all these things will be given to you as well.

1 Peter 3:15

But in your hearts revere Christ as Lord. Always be prepared to give an answer to everyone who asks you to give the reason for the hope that you have. But do this with gentleness and respect.

A Process for Planning: PLOW

I'm not a farmer, but I did find something interesting in the field of agriculture. It was a website, sponsored by De Dell Seeds, that gave famers tips on how to improve their corn crop. Nine practical suggestions were made, including "Weed Early and Often," "Ensure Proper Water Drainage," and "Plant Early, Plant Effectively."[19]

While my farming knowledge is limited, I'm guessing these are some good observations for farmers to do better. What's true with growing crops is also true with growing people for the kingdom of Christ. To grow spiritual fruit the teacher must:

1. Focus on the meaning of the Bible truth.
2. Involve students in an active search for that truth.
3. Stimulate and guide learners in the process of discovery.[20]

That's our goal. How do we get there? We must plow. I can see that you're puzzled. We're aren't harnessing the horses and headed out to the field. The acronym "PLOW" will clarify the components of planning or preparing for success.

---

19   "9 Ways To Improve Corn Crop Yields: A Farmer's Guide," https://www.dedellseeds.com/resource/9-ways-improve-corn-crop-yields/

20   Richards, *Christian Education: Foundations for the Future* p. 172.

This method is appropriate for all levels of preparation. From preparing a new class, choosing a curriculum, setting up an event or teaching a class, "PLOW" will help.

Pray

Before starting any activity, we must bathe it in prayer. Prayer is an indispensable step in the ladder of success. We know there's power in prayer. Max Lucado writes about that power as he notes, "Prayer changes things because prayer appeals to the top power in the universe. Prayer is not a magical formula or a mystical chant. It is the yes to God's invitation to invoke his name."[21]

The Bible has quite a bit to say about prayer.

Philippians 4:6

Do not be anxious about anything, but in every situation, by prayer and petition, with thanksgiving, present your requests to God.

1 John 5:14

This is the confidence we have in approaching God: that if we ask anything according to his will, he hears us.

Ephesians 6:18

And pray in the Spirit on all occasions with all kinds of prayers and requests. With this in mind, be alert and always keep on praying for all the Lord's people.

Luke 18:1

Then Jesus told his disciples a parable to show them that they should always pray and not give up.

At this point, you might be asking, "why put so much emphasis on prayer?" There are three important reasons why prayer ought to be the starting point as we endeavor to do anything for the kingdom.

---

21 Lucado, Max, *Before Amen*, Thomas Nelson, Nashville, 2014, p. 98.

First, as we begin preparation for whatever we may be doing, prayer is what engages the Holy Spirit and our spirit. Whatever plan we make, needs to be the plan God has for us. There's truth in the anonymous adage, "Those who leave everything in God's hand will eventually see God's hand in everything." Prayer allows us the opportunity to pay attention to the promptings of God's Spirit. Whatever good we accomplish will not be done by own our strength or ingenuity. As Zechariah wrote in Zechariah 4:6, ""This is the word of the Lord to Zerubbabel: 'Not by might nor by power, but by my Spirit,' says the Lord Almighty."

Martin Luther knew the connection between accomplishment and prayer. Luther was known as a prayer warrior. He's said to have written, "I have so much to do that I shall have to spend the first three hours in prayer!"[22]

Additionally, prayer can align our thoughts and dreams to match what God's will is for a given situation. What may seem like a wonderful idea on paper, may be revealed to be the desire of our own heart and not God's. The leading of the Holy Spirit gives us the opportunity to discern that. Prayer opens the door for the Holy Spirit to interact with us. Billy Graham was asked, "How can I tell if God is telling me to do something?" His answer was direct. "Pray about the decisions you make; ask if what you're seeking is honoring to Christ."[23]

Finally, it's through prayer that we can have the confidence to do what God's called us to do. Wanting to align our will with God's and involving the Holy Spirit in that process leads to the assurance that we are doing what God wants. Jeremiah 33:3 says, "Call to me and I will answer you and tell you great and unsearchable things you do not know." Drawing near to God and allowing the Holy Spirit to direct our paths helps provide the confidence we need to accomplish what's before us.

22 C.H. Spurgeon, "Degrees of Power Attending the Gospel," A Sermon Delivered on Sunday Morning, September 3, 1865, https://www.spurgeongems.org/vols10-12/chs648.pdf

23 Billy Graham, "Answers," Billy Graham Evangelistic Association, November 22, 2011, https://billygraham.org/answer/how-can-i-tell-if-god-is-telling-me-to-do-something-or-if-im-just-imagining-it-must-be-ok-with-god-but-it-isnt/

List

The second component of the process of planning is to list. That sounds like a simple thing, doesn't it? In a way, it is. What does it mean to list? After praying and seeking what God wants us to do regarding whatever it might be we're preparing, is make a list of different options or methods to accomplish that task. While listing ideas can be done individually, it's better when it's a group effort. Listing options in a group setting is often called brainstorming.

For example, perhaps you are leading a student ministry. You've felt led to have a Friday night event in the fall after football games. You've spent time praying about it and seeking whether this is really what the Lord wants you to do. You're confident that it is. What's the next step?

Bring in a group of creative, trusted people (volunteers or staff) to sit with you and brainstorm how you might accomplish having this Friday night event. List the various ideas and approaches. During this time in the process, there are no bad ideas. List them all and encourage your creative team to give as many as they can.

Why does making a list matter? Listing and brainstorming with a group allows for ideas to be brought up and examined in a cooperative way. The result of this kind of collaborative effort can lead to discovering the best approach to accomplish something.

There are some important things to keep in mind during this process.

1. Choose wisely the people you involve in the creative/ brainstorming process. Nothing will get accomplished if the creative group is full of people who are not on board with your ministry or who do not see the same broad vision you do. You don't want your creative team filled with people who just think every idea you have is a great one. However, you also don't want the group to be filled with people who oppose what you're trying to do. Prayerfully choose those people who can dream big things and those who can provide

constructive criticism and can winnow through bad ideas to find better ones.

2. Recognize that brainstorming is designed for idea volume, not depth or quality. This process will not give you or your group the detailed methodology to implement what you believe you're called to do. This part of the process is to see how many ways the goal can be accomplished, and which ideas are unworkable.

3. Learn to facilitate this kind of session. You'll want to encourage ideas and creativity while fighting the temptation for the group to get off track or to land on one idea too early. Learn how to ask open-ended questions that stimulate thinking.

4. Remember that generating ideas is a small part of the process. This part of the process matters and shouldn't be overlooked, but it is not the result. The ideas that emerge from your listing/brainstorming session will move to the next stage.

Let's go back to our fictional Friday night idea. Your listing/brainstorming session might have produced a list that looks like this...

- Have students come to the student minister's house.
- Have the students gather at a different house each Friday.
- Have the students meet at church.
- Have the event be something like a lock-in.
- Have a dance for the kids.
- Have music, video games and let the kids hang out.
- Try to get the school to allow us to use the gym for an event that includes sports.
- Meet with the students at the local pizza place.

This is merely a sample of what a brainstorming/listing session might produce. Being able to dream ideas and list different ways to get something done can be fun. It can be a time for vision casting and expansion. It can be a time for team-building and encouragement. It's an important time. What comes next?

Optimize

The third step of the process is to optimize. That's not a verb that gets used a lot. What does it mean? To optimize means to make something the best it can be. Once you've gone through the brainstorming and listing process, you (and possibly your group) must select the best way to accomplish your goal. The winnowing down of ideas to the best one, is an optimization procedure.

This isn't a revolutionary idea. It's simply choosing the best idea and working to make that idea as good as it can be. This process can be done alone, but it's often better to involve a small group of people (not necessarily the same creative group). Some of the optimization process may be intuitive, but there are some principles that can assist in taking a good idea and making it great.

1. Develop a detailed plan or course of action. Write it out; allowing each person on the team to comment. If you are planning an event, describe it from the promotional phase through the end of the event.

2. Focus on the specific plan. Look at it through the lens of details and explanations. Have your small group analyze it as if they were a parent, asking every question imaginable.

3. Tweak and adjust the plan as a result of your focus. Are there things that could be done better? Is there something that is inherently problematic? This is the time to go from good to better or better to best.

4. Leave the plan on your desk. You and your group pray. Make certain that what you're about to do is what God wants you to do.

5. Affirm, after a time of prayer, that this is the course of action.

Let's return to our previous example. You are a student minister and you're planning to do a Friday event after the football games in your town. You've made a list of all the ways you could do this. After the optimization process, you've decided to have an event at the church. It will be on Friday nights, from 9:00 until 11:30. You are going to have pizza and sodas. You'll have snack-type foods, too. You'll set up the church's video games in the student center. Music will be playing. It will be an informal gathering of students. You'll have no less than four adult chaperones each Friday. You've established that you'll give each student a wristband who comes. If they leave, they are not allowed to come back in. You'll have a short devotion at ten o'clock. There won't be a charge because you have some people in church who'll provide money for each Friday.

That's the detailed plan. Your group has analyzed it from every possible angle to make sure everything is covered. You've prayed about it and are convinced this is the way to go. What do you do next?

Wrap

The last component of the planning process is what I call "wrap." The phrase "that's a wrap" is a colloquial expression that indicates everything appears to be satisfactory.[24] In the context of the planning process it's used as a verb meaning to bring it all together. Maybe a more simple way to say it would be "get it done."

The last part of the preparation part is to simply do it. Implement the plan. We need to take to heart Jesus' words in Mark 10:45. He said, "For even the Son of Man did not come to be served, but to serve, and to give his life as a ransom for many." We are called to work. Peter writes in 1 Peter 4:10, "Each of you should use whatever gift you have received to serve others, as faithful stewards of God's grace in its various forms."

---

24 *Urban Dictionary*, https://www.urbandictionary.com/define.php?term=wrap

Make it happen. Just do it. There are lots of ways to express the same idea. We must do what God has called us to do. There are three crucial things we need to remember.

1. Bring excitement and enthusiasm to what you're doing. If you can't be excited about it, who will be? Enthusiasm is contagious, so be the carrier.

2. Have things ready when they are supposed to be ready. Nothing says "not that important" as something that is being thrown together at the last minute. While some details may have slipped or last-minute corrections might have to happen, that shouldn't be the norm.

3. Have fun. This is vital. What we're doing is important, but it ought to be something we enjoy. If we're working with students or kids, this is obvious, but even with adults, there needs to be something intrinsically enjoyable about what we're doing.

Implementing the plan is the fun part, the celebration of the long process of preparation. You've been called by the Lord to work for him. The harvest is plentiful, but the workers are few. You've answered the call. You've put your hand to the plow. No looking back. "PLOW;" that's what you've done. The plan is in place and it's happening. What comes next?

Evaluation

The plan is in place and we're doing it. That leads to the question, "How well are we doing it?" That question comes from the well called "evaluation." Evaluations sometimes cause panic or fear. There are quite a few people who don't like the idea of evaluations. The truth is, though, most people have evaluations all the time.

For the student, evaluation comes in the form of an exam. For the artist, evaluation comes in the reviews of the critics. For the athlete and coach, evaluation is seen in terms of the final score. For business owners, the evaluation is measured in terms of business volume. Evaluation isn't really something to be dreaded. It's a tool that can help us do even better.

The Bible tells us why we need to evaluate what we do. "For my thoughts are not your thoughts, neither are your ways my ways," declares the Lord. As the heavens are higher than the earth, so are my ways higher than your ways and my thoughts than your thoughts" (Isaiah 55:8-9). James writes in James 1:5, "If any of you lacks wisdom, you should ask God, who gives generously to all without finding fault, and it will be given to you." As we look at evaluation, we'll examine four important questions; who, how, when and why.

Who?

The first question regarding evaluation is who should be evaluating. We understand what it is we're evaluating, the plan, the program, or the event. The question is who the evaluator should be. The answer to that is clear. The one who is responsible for the program is ultimately responsible for the evaluation of it.

In the practical sense, an evaluation is often done by a supervisor. Someone who is higher on the responsibility chart usually assesses those below him/her. Reality also suggests that those whom we serve will do an informal evaluation. The things they like and approve of are well attended and supported. The things they don't like or care for, often are ignored, unsupported and left to die on the vine. Evaluations done by a supervisor and those done by constituents are important and ought to be examined. However, that doesn't excuse us from doing our own evaluations. We must evaluate what we do if we're going to be as effective as we ought to be.

Here are five observations regarding evaluating our own ministry or program.

1. Commit to an honest assessment. It's easy to allow ourselves a bit of a break. After all, we know our intentions and they were good. This, however, doesn't help. Make sure you take an honest look at what you're doing.

2. Reflect on what you see. An honest evaluation allows us a firsthand look at how well what we intended to happen did take place. No one knows better than we do what we set out to do, so no one is in a better place to check its effectiveness.

3. Identify and define specific areas of needed improvement. While some programs do excellent work, no one program is perfect. Find ways you can improve.

4. Identify and define specific areas you do well. Encouragement matters and noting what goes right is a positive thing for you and your team.

5. Share your assessment with teammates or a supervisor. This adds a layer of accountability, especially the intent to improve.

The bottom line is that you are responsible to evaluate and improve your program.

How?

The next question then, is how do I do that? I know I ought to check the health and success of what I'm doing, but how do I do it? Again, commit to the five principles noted in the paragraph above. Too many times, people have deluded themselves because they rejected an honest evaluation. Once I'm there, though, what's next?

There are several different approaches to doing this and an online search will show you lots of options. Here are what I think are the foundational principles.

1. Gather accurate data. This means evaluate the effectiveness of a ministry after an appropriate amount of time. Try to ascertain knowable facts. How many times did the group meet? How many people attended? How many volunteers were involved? How many different people did the ministry affect? Were there any decisions to follow Christ made in this ministry?

Combine this empirical data with subjective information. What were some of the comments made by the students who came? What were the responses of your volunteers?

2. Interpret the data in an honest way. Look at the numbers. While the church is more than numbers, numbers do tell a story. Evaluate what the people who were involved said about the program. Try to write and present an accurate depiction of what the data shows.

3. Compare the goals and mission of the ministry with what actually took place in the allotted time period. Did the ministry accomplish what it ought to have? Were the goals realistic? Do they need to be adjusted or scrapped?

4. Assess if you had the right amount of help or if the help you had was sufficiently trained to accomplish what you planned to accomplish. Perhaps, if you are doing small groups, your volunteers need more small group training.

5. Determine if adjustments are needed to make the ministry program more effective or if the ministry program should continue. Perhaps the ministry can continue as it is without change. Whichever is the case, this is the time when that determination is first stated.

6. Pray and see what the Lord may have to say about what your initial thoughts are.

7. Celebrate the successes you had, even if the ministry will not continue. People want to know that what they did mattered. Share with your people (volunteers and those who attended) the good things that happened.

8. Decide to make the appropriate changes and do it.

Evaluations are hard, but necessary. It's tough to do them. It's always hard to see a ministry program end. It's hard to have to adjust. However, no program remains relevant and effective without some change. Winston Churchill once said, "There is nothing wrong in change, if it is in the right direction. To improve is to change, so to be perfect is to have changed often."[25] We can't be afraid of making changes. Too many times ministries grow cold and ineffective because they've avoided evaluation and appropriate change.

When?

After establishing that evaluation matters, that we ought to do them and seeing how they are to be done, the next question is when. At what point in the life of this ministry or program should I initiate evaluation?

It's an important question. If evaluation is done too soon, the results will be invalid and any assessment premature. If evaluation is done too late, then it may not be able to help or improve a particular ministry. It's a bit like Goldilocks and the Three Bears. The porridge can't be too hot or too cold. It must be just right. That's how it is with the timing of evaluation.

Each ministry is different, and as such, should be handled in an individual manner. Some ministries may be able to be assessed after a few months while others may require a full year to get a proper perspective. What is best is to set an evaluation time as the ministry launches and determine, as that time nears, whether it is the right time. Here are four suggestions that will help determine when an evaluation is appropriate.

1. As the ministry is happening, collect data. Make notes of how each group meeting goes. Note the attendance and, to the best of your ability, ascertain the mood of those who attended. Was it a positive experience? Did you get the sense that what you did that night mattered?

2. Gather feedback continually from your volunteers and those who attend. Simply put, talk to your people. You don't have to have a formalized set of questions but listen to them to get a general idea of how it's going. This will give you insight into when a more formal evaluation is necessary.

25   James C. Humes, *The Wit and Wisdom of Winston Churchill*, Harper Collins, 2009, p. 288

3. Create a list of open-ended questions to check the health of what you are doing. Keep in mind the mission of the ministry and how it connects to the larger mission of the group. Create the list as you do the ministry. The urgency of the list will help you determine when an evaluation is needed.

4. Set a time, either midway through your ministry if it is time governed one, or after a few months, to meet with your volunteers and go over the questions. Invite some of your team members who may not be a part of this ministry to sit in and listen.

The general manager of the Oakland Athletics Billy Beane once said, "We've got to use every piece of data and piece of information, and hopefully that will help us be accurate with our player evaluation. For us, that's our life blood."[26] Evaluation is not only the lifeblood of baseball teams, it's the lifeblood of ministry success, too.

Why?

Evaluation is essential. We understand that in nearly every area of our lives. People go to the doctor and the dentist for regular checkups. If we want our cars to run well, we take them in at the right time for oil changes and maintenance. We get online to check our bank accounts and pay our bills. Students and occasionally parents will check grades and assignments online. We do these things consistently to make sure that everything is going well. Ministry is no different. Ministries cannot survive and thrive without regular checkups.

There are some benefits that come from evaluating. You can …

1. Build a culture of success — You can have tangible things to celebrate with your team and your people. Celebrating success matters and that celebration needs to be genuine or people will see through it. A real evaluation will give you the basis for celebration.

26 Michael Lewis, *Moneyball: The Art of Winning an Unfair Game*, W.W. Norton and Co, (2004).

2. Develop the gifts and skills of your team — Evaluation will reveal areas of strength and areas where a person might need to improve. You can gain valuable insight and better train people when this information is available to you.

3. Keep the main thing the main thing — This might be the most important of the benefits. We do ministry because we love Jesus and want others to know and love him, too. Evaluation of a ministry or activity, if done well, will show us how well that's being done and if it is emphasized as much as it ought to be. A ministry can have lots of good things going on, but still not accomplish the primary reason it exists. Evaluation is crucial in that.

The principle of Proverbs 27:17, I think, speaks to the importance of evaluation. "As iron sharpens iron, so one person sharpens another." Evaluation makes ministry and us better.

Questions for Reflection

1. In the first part of this chapter, the importance of planning is discussed. What are some hindrances to planning? What makes planning indispensable for ministry?

2. The first part of the acronym "PLOW" is to pray. That seems obvious and yet it isn't done as often or effectively as it could be. Why do you think prayer is neglected?

3. The second part of "PLOW" is to list. The chapter asserts that listing is like a brainstorming session. What are some strengths you see of doing this? What might be some weaknesses?

4. The third part of "PLOW" is to optimize. The chapter notes that optimization is the making the chosen idea better. Having read the chapter, why might this

be important? How much time do you think ought to be devoted to this?

5. The last part of "PLOW" is the "wrap" or getting it done. After reading the chapter, do you think this is a challenge for leaders? Do some people go to this step without the rest of "PLOW?" Is that a good thing? Why or why not?

6. Explain your view of evaluation and why it matters. How will you utilize evaluation in your ministry?

Chapter 3

Staffing and Motivation

One of the most challenging aspects of Christian Education administration is finding enough volunteers to staff your program and motivating them to keep at it. Is there anything more important to the success of your ministry than the quality of the volunteer team that you're able to recruit? Is there anything more vital than keeping your team enthused and engaged in what you're doing?

The answer to both questions is a resounding "Yes," but while we see the importance of it, the actual implementation is much harder. What do we do to better recruit capable people? Are there things we can do to inspire and challenge our current team? How do we deal with burnout among our volunteer staff? This chapter takes a close and practical look at these real issues for those who administrate Christian Education ministries.

The Most Coveted Asset of the Church: The Volunteer

What is a volunteer and why does he or she matter? A volunteer is someone who sees value and importance in a particular task and wants to dedicate himself/herself to assist doing that task. The reason why volunteers matter? "Successful ministry in a church depends upon the recruitment and development of many leaders who freely give their services."[27]

For most people who've been in and/or worked in a church, this comes as no surprise. There isn't a church, large or small, that doesn't depend on the work of volunteers to accomplish what they do. Volunteers are a valuable, precious commodity.

I'm a baseball card collector. I've been doing that since I was in the second grade. I used to love the look at them al-

---

27 Jerry M. Stubblefield, *Christian Education Handbook*, ed. Bruce Powers, B & H Publishers, 1996, p. 81

most every day and play games with them on the floor of our living room. At some point in my early teen years, I realized that they could be valuable if they were kept in good condition. I began doing that. The best cards I have are a 1956 Jackie Robinson card and a 1964 Sandy Koufax card. I enjoy these two cards and all of them, really. I won't be selling them. I'm sure someday, someone else will have that task. The "Holy Grail" for baseball card collectors, though, isn't either one of these. It's a 1909 Honus Wagner card. This 1909 American Tobacco Company card remains the symbol of trading card collecting today. Even in poor condition, they routinely sell for over $1 million.[28]

That's incredible! To find something as rare and valuable as that would be an amazing treasure. I'm convinced that what we're looking for in volunteers for ministry is the equivalent of the Honus Wagner card. When you find that remarkable volunteer, it's worth more than others can imagine.

So, how do we do that? What are some things we can do to find that rare, precious gem, the wonderful, all-purpose volunteer? Here are some thoughts about recruiting:

1. Pray and ask God to bring people into your sphere that have a heart and passion to serve. It's important that the volunteers we bring in have the heart for it and are wanting to serve God in that way. (1 Peter 4:10-11)

2. Establish a principle that your volunteers will have a walk with Jesus Christ and show some evidence of the fruit of the Spirit in their lives. This has to be a non-negotiable issue. Your leaders can't lead when they don't know where they're going.

3. Develop a list or file of potential leaders and keep it updated. When someone new comes to your church, talk to them. Find out if they have any interest, passion or gifts in your ministry area. Keep the list current and pray for the people on it.

---

28 "100 Most Valuable Baseball Cards in 2019: The Complete List," *Odd Sports Cards*, https://www.oldsportscards.com/most-valuable-baseball-cards/

4. Don't ask for "warm bodies" to fill a spot. Seek passionate, gifted people and challenge them that this is a way they can serve God. Christians generally want to do things for the Lord, but don't often know how to make it happen. Make sure that you present the opportunity in your ministry as more than just filling a role. Let them see it as fulfilling a calling.

5. Don't compromise maturity or wisdom when getting volunteers to teach. It isn't better just to have someone. Teachers are held to a higher standard (James 3:1), so make sure those you have teaching/leading are those who are ready and trained.

6. Talk to people personally. Jesus did that (Matthew 4:18-20) and we should, too. Show an interest in the person and that you value them by talking to them in person.

7. Do a background check on every volunteer without exception.

8. Meet with volunteer candidates in person. Don't just accept new people without personally knowing something about him/her.

What the Bible says about Serving

William Penn once said, "I expect to pass through life but once. If, therefore, there be any kindness I can show, or any good thing I can do to any fellow-being, let me do it now, and not defer or neglect it, as I shall not pass this way again."[29] We understand that sentiment. The Bible is clear about the challenge of serving.

Hebrews 6:10-12

God is not unjust; he will not forget your work and the love you have shown him as you have helped his people and continue to help them. We want each of you to show this same diligence to

---

29 William Penn, Forbes Quotes; *Thoughts on the Business of Life*, https://www.forbes. com/quotes/10118/

the very end, so that what you hope for may be fully realized. We do not want you to become lazy, but to imitate those who through faith and patience inherit what has been promised.

Matthew 28:11-12

The greatest among you will be your servant. For those who exalt themselves will be humbled, and those who humble themselves will be exalted.

Romans 12:9-13

Love must be sincere. Hate what is evil; cling to what is good. Be devoted to one another in love. Honor one another above yourselves. Never be lacking in zeal, but keep your spiritual fervor, serving the Lord. Be joyful in hope, patient in affliction, faithful in prayer. Share with the Lord's people who are in need. Practice hospitality.

Ephesians 2:8-10

For it is by grace you have been saved, through faith — and this is not from yourselves, it is the gift of God — not by works, so that no one can boast. For we are God's handiwork, created in Christ Jesus to do good works, which God prepared in advance for us to do.

Isaiah 6:8

Then I heard the voice of the Lord saying, "Whom shall I send? And who will go for us?" And I said, "Here am I. Send me."

Training Volunteers for Success

Once we have a good team of volunteers, the next step is training them to be successful in the ministry. Mark Senter wrote, "No matter how many other things I do well in my role as minister of Christian education, if I fail to obtain and develop capable teachers and leaders to do the work of discipleship throughout the educational ministries of the church, everything else is window dressing."[30] One of the most important things we do as Christian leaders, is equip our teammates for success.

God has equipped the people around us in the body of Christ. The writer of Hebrews notes this as we read, "Now may the God of peace, who through the blood of the eternal covenant brought back from the dead our Lord Jesus, that great Shepherd of the sheep, equip you with everything good for doing his will, and may he work in us what is pleasing to him, through Jesus Christ, to whom be glory for ever and ever" (Hebrews 13:20-21). It's our responsibility to get out of them what God has put in them. How do we do that?

1. Don't compromise that your volunteers must have a relationship with Jesus Christ. You can teach lots of skills and techniques, but a relationship with Jesus isn't something that can be taught. Your volunteer must be a Christian.

2. Know and communicate clearly what the ministry role you're wanting the volunteer to fill entails.

3. Work with your volunteer(s) to establish what his/her strengths and weaknesses are. Be sure to challenge the volunteer to try to go one step further than he or she thinks he or she can go.

4. Explain in detail what you want the volunteer to do and to accomplish. Make sure that he/she knows what is expected and what the "rules" are of your particular ministry.

5. Establish an appropriate communication system with your volunteer. Make sure they know you're there to assist them. Make sure they understand how you expect the different aspects of communication to happen and what accountability they have.

6. Once they understand what is expected and the accountability that's in place, allow them the space to do

---

30 Mark Senter, "Understanding and Using Curriculum," *Christian Education: Foundations for the Future*, ed. Robert E. Clark, Moody, 1991, p. 469.

the work. Let them bring their own creative abilities and passions to the task. If they do something the way that you demand it, they may get proficient at doing your program. If you give them the space to use their own talents, they may create a wonderful program that they have a stake in.

Training and teaching volunteers is important. It is often the difference between a successful ministry and one that's struggling.

Lorri Freifeld wrote in *Training* magazine, "These last few months certainly have been trying times. Mother Nature unleashed her fury in Hurricanes Harvey, Irma, Maria, and Nate and the devastating earthquake in Mexico. Wildfires scorched more than 200,000 acres of land and decimated 5,000-plus structures in California. Man added to the heartbreak with the shooting spree in Las Vegas. Tragically, many lives were lost in all of these instances, and my heart aches for all those who suffered the loss of family and friends. But many other lives were saved — by the bravery, grit, and, yes, training of the people on the scene."[31]

I'm not suggesting that training volunteers at church is a life or death situation (though I can certainly see the case for training people in the case of an intruder coming into the church that might be a bit more of a life issue), but it matters.

What do our volunteers wish we knew?

Before we get too far in analyzing our volunteers and how to get the most from them, it might be good for us to consider what our volunteers might be wanting from us. Here are three important things that, I believe, volunteers want church leaders to remember.

1. They want to know that what they're doing matters in the big picture. This is important. No one signs up to do something irrelevant. There are some tasks that are naturally more upfront or noticeable than others.

---

31 Lorri Freifeld, "Training Really Does Matter," *Training*,
   Link: https://trainingmag.com/trgmag-article/training-really-does-matter/

However, we have to show how what we ask a volunteer to do contributes to the big picture of reaching your group's goal or mission.

2. They want us to remember that they need breaks. If we're honest, we know that we need, from time to time, to get away from what we're doing. There's a temptation, though, once we get a quality volunteer to consider giving them a lifetime appointment. While many may serve multiple years, everyone enjoys some time off. This is easy on paper, but it's tough.

   It's been my experience that scheduling breaks is hard. You'll have many teachers who've taught for a long time and will want to continue to do so. At the other end of the spectrum, you'll have people who'll only want to commit to serving once a month. It isn't realistic to think you're going to be able to give a teacher a random, full month off, but you'll want to allow them the opportunity to be gone some throughout the year and utilize a substitute. Just be in tune with the fact that, though it may be expressed in different ways, we all need a break from time to time.

3. They need and want to be appreciated. This is true of all of us. We want to know that what we've done matters. I don't know that anyone serves for that reason but letting them know that they're a valuable member of the team is important.

Keeping in mind what our volunteers are looking for in us will help us get all that God has put in them.

Can you ever learn enough?

Once we have a system in place to train the new volunteers we pray for and God brings us, is that it? Is there any additional training needed?

Continued learning is crucial to the ongoing success of a ministry. Lots of ministries start off with a bang and are doing great, only to, after a few months, lose their spark and energy.

They begin to go through motions on their way to the grave-yard of ministry failures. If leaders and volunteers continue to learn more and implement new, fresh ideas in existing ministries, the lifecycle for that ministry is extended. What are some things you can do to create an environment of continued learning and growth? Here are some suggestions.

1. Utilize social media to send a short devotional thought or teaching tip to your whole team on a weekly basis. Doing this will allow your whole team to have a common ground on which you can discuss things. It will also give you an opportunity to challenge and stimulate them as you feel the Holy Spirit leading you.

2. Have regular meeting times. I want to give a warning here. No one is particularly fond of more meetings. So, it's imperative that this not just be "another meeting." Set a specific time, maybe less than an hour, and honor it. Have a specific agenda and make sure you include a time of celebrating success and giving deeper scriptural or spiritual insight. Whether you do this quarterly, monthly, or bi-monthly, plan it well.

3. Provide a list of quality books, blogs and websites you find encouraging to your volunteers. Make sure you give them access to some of the amazing stuff that fills your cup.

4. Plan once a year or every two years to attend a professional training session. Many of the publishing companies put these on in connection with a VBS curriculum or a convention. Sometimes nearby Christian colleges will have programs like this. Find out what's in your area and engage with it to some degree.

5. Make sure that your volunteers see in you a passion and hunger to know and grow more. That spirit is contagious, so let them see it in you. Never quit learning and growing yourself.

A.W. Tozer once said, "The stiff and wooden quality about our religious lives is a result of our lack of holy desire. Complacency is a deadly foe of all spiritual growth. Acute desire must be present or there will be no manifestation of Christ to his people."[32] Simply put, you have to have to "want" to grow and know more.

Motivation

The Difference and Connection between Motivation and Inspiration

How a leader can challenge a member of his or her team to want to do more, give more or perform even better is a hard thing. From the sports arena to the classroom, there are debates about how a coach or teacher can motivate. There is a distinction between motivation and inspiration. Generally, a person can't be motivated by someone else. "Motivation is internal, not external."[33] So, if it's true that we can't motivate someone else, do we just leave it at that?

While that would lead to a shorter chapter, the answer is no. There are some things we, as leaders, coaches, or teachers, can do that will foster motivation. While we don't motivate, by definition, we can and should inspire. When we inspire people, we are calling them to look beyond the immediate situation to what can be. Inspiration compels people to look within themselves to see if they have more to give to accomplish what is set before them. Inspiration provides a reason or rationale for people to unleash the passion and fire that burns within them. Inspiration fuels motivation.

"There is no magic formula church leaders can follow to inspire others. What causes one person to respond positively may generate a negative response from another."[34] Inspiring people is not an exact science. There isn't a checklist of things to do each time that will lead to a person being fired

---

32 A.W. Tozer, "Christian Quotes," https://www.christianquotes.info/top-quotes/17-inspiring-quotes-about-learning-and-growing/

33 Jerry M. Stubblefield, *Christian Education Handbook*, ed. Bruce Powers, B & H Publishers, 1996, p. 94.

34 Stubblefield, *Ibid.* p. 94.

up to do something great. When a person is inspired, motivation follows.

Motivation matters. It helps us keep going when things are hard. It pushes us through times of failure. Michael Jordan, NBA all-star, once said, "I've failed over and over again in my life. And that is why I succeed."[35] Great leaders are able to inspire and challenge others to be even better. That's at the heart of why some consider Michael Jordan to be the greatest basketball player ever. He made those who played with him better.[36]

I don't want to get into the argument of who is the greatest basketball player ever, though I might have an opinion or two. The key is to inspire to foster motivation. Don't give in to failure and don't accept "good enough."

Biblical Texts on Motivation

Inspiring and encouraging teammates is not just a sports thing. There is a biblical precedent for encouraging those around us, especially those with whom we work.

Proverbs 17:17

A friend loves at all times, and a brother is born for a time of adversity.

Isaiah 40:28-31

Do you not know? Have you not heard? The Lord is the everlasting God, the Creator of the ends of the earth. He will not grow tired or weary, and his understanding no one can fathom. He gives strength to the weary and increases the power of the weak. Even youths grow tired and weary, and young men stumble and fall; but those who hope in the Lord will renew their strength. They will soar on wings like eagles; they will run and not grow weary; they will walk and not be faint.

35 Jacob Cashman, "Sports Quotes to Get You Going." https://www.lifehack.org/294074/15-inspirational-sports-quotes-get-you-going

36 Fox Doucette, "LeBron James, Michael Jordan, and "Making Teammates Better," *Pace and Space*, March 16, 2019. http://paceandspacehoops.com/lebron-james-michael-jordan-and-making-teammates-better/

Hebrews 10:23-25

Let us hold unswervingly to the hope we profess, for he who promised is faithful. And let us consider how we may spur one another on toward love and good deeds, not giving up meeting together, as some are in the habit of doing, but encouraging one another — and all the more as you see the Day approaching.

1 Thessalonians 5:11

Therefore encourage one another and build each other up, just as in fact you are doing.

Ecclesiastes 4:9-12

Two are better than one, because they have a good return for their labor: If either of them falls down, one can help the other up. But pity anyone who falls and has no one to help them up. Also, if two lie down together, they will keep warm. But how can one keep warm alone? Though one may be overpowered, two can defend themselves. A cord of three strands is not quickly broken.

Creating a Climate Where Motivation Flourishes

How can we set up our ministry in such a way that our people are motivated? Here are some characteristics of a motivation inspiring culture.

1. Trust — Motivation thrives in the soil of trust. The challenge for leaders is to develop a trusting relationship. If I am to "spur" someone else on to "love and good deeds," then my words to them must ring true and they must trust that I will speak and deal honestly with them. Stephen Covey writes, "Truth is the highest form of human motivation. It brings out the very best in people."[37] People respond well to those with whom they've developed a trusting relationship. The coach whose been with his or her players through the

---

37 Stephen R. Covey, *The 7 Habits of Highly Successful People: Powerful Lessons in Personal Change*, Simon and Schuster, New York, 1989, p. 178

ups and downs of a grueling season has likely built a wall of trust that can inspire his/her players and compel them to a greater level of motivation.

Take time to develop trust relationships. Demonstrate integrity in the relationships you have with those around you. "Speak the truth in love" (Ephesians 4:15) as you interact with those who work with you.

2. Pray — In the realm of ministry, the goal is greater than just winning the game. We are part of a kingdom over which the gates of hell will not prevail. Helping our team see the eternal significance of what we're doing is the inspiration that can lead to motivation. The vision for what can be comes from the Holy Spirit working in the hearts of those who work with us. Pray for each volunteer and ask God to encourage, bless and inspire them.

It seems as if prayer makes an appearance in every chapter. If so, that's a good thing. 1 Timothy 2:1 says, "I urge, then, first of all, that petitions, prayers, intercession and thanksgiving be made for all people." Intercede on behalf of your team. Pray that God will allow the Holy Spirit to show them possibilities and opportunities that can ignite a passionate flame of work and service.

3. Honest Praise — Hardly anything is more inspiring that genuine praise and recognition. Seek out the things your volunteers do right and let them know about it. We all like words of affirmation and congratulations. Celebrate the successes publicly.

I was the chaplain for a high school football team a few years ago. I hope they learned a bit from me, but I know I learned from them. One of the lessons that has stuck with me is the way they celebrated success. I did a devotional or character talk each Monday and Thursday during the team meeting. On Monday, right before my talk, they gave out the weekend awards.

Win or lose, the coach recognized players for exceptional work the previous game and week. They had designated "official" awards for the team (a giant sledgehammer for the defensive player of the week was most memorable to me). Though I do remember a few awards, what I mostly remember was the united sense of excitement that embodied that part of the week. Players were inspired to dig deeper and do even more. I've tried to duplicate that (not so much the sledgehammer), in the ministries I've had.

Celebration of success is important. Again, it has to be real and based in truth. They didn't give out a defensive player of the week if there wasn't one but celebrating real wins matter. Nothing inspires more motivation than being a contributing member of a team that's doing something special.

4. Honest Criticism — When the need comes for constructive criticism or even confrontation, don't shirk from it. People respect those who address things head on and it can be a factor in inspiring a change in behavior. It is important, though, how you approach this. Remember Ephesians 4:15 which says, "Instead, speaking the truth in love, we will grow to become in every respect the mature body of him who is the head, that is, Christ."

Be honest when you have to confront your team members and do so from the background of demonstrating your love for them and your desire that they grow and mature, even from their mistakes.

There are some good principles to follow when you must deal with problems. First, praise in public and correct in private. This is an important policy to follow in almost every area of your ministry and life. Second, don't only focus on the negative. That's an easy thing to do and if the volunteer hasn't done anything positive, then you and they have bigger issues. Let them know what you appreciate. Address clearly and specifically the areas that were not done or handled correctly. Allow the volunteer to respond. Perhaps there is something you don't know about the situation that might change your view of it. Once you've stated what you've seen and they've responded, if there is a corrective measure, state it. Finally, begin the process of aiming the volunteer for success by noting that you still believe in him or her and that you know things will work better. Before you end a confrontation time, pray about the situation and for your volunteer.

There are also those occasions when you must have a "hard talk" with a volunteer about how you no longer need their work. In the business world, this is called "being fired." We don't, however, fire volunteers, but you do, from time to time, have to let someone know that it isn't working out. How do you do that? First, as always, pray. Pray for the person and the conversation you're about to have. Second, meet with them in person. Don't send a text or an email. Be upfront and speak in person. Third, give what praise you can give. Fourth, get right to the point. Say something like, "God equips all of us differently. You have gifts and talents, but they just don't seem to be a good match for this ministry." Don't sugarcoat it or dance around it. Say it. Allow them a chance to respond and then offer to help them or direct them to the person who can help them find a new ministry in which they can serve. It isn't easy, but doing it well helps your ministry and the ministry of the entire church.

5. Cast a Vision — In Philippians 4, Paul lists all the things he's faced in his life, both good and bad. He's been through the ups and downs of life. His conclusion is found in verse 13. He says, "I can do all this through him who gives me strength." That's the

mindset or vision that will lead to a successful ministry. No matter what happens, good or bad, we can do all things, not because of our own strength, wisdom or ability, but through Jesus who empowers and enables us. As I see it, there can be no more important focal point than that.

Having a vision or goal to aim for matters. It matters for teams of all kinds. We see it most often in sports.

At Notre Dame, there is a sign every member of the Fighting Irish slaps as he's coming onto the field. The sign says, "Play Like A Champion Today." There's an interesting story behind that sign. It was originally created by Laurie Wenger who used to work in the Notre Dame sign shop. Lou Holtz was the new football coach at Notre Dame in 1986. One day, he was leafing through an old football picture book and saw a black-and-white picture of a sign that said, "Play Like a Champion Today." He had to have one. It was the vision for his time at Notre Dame. He sent an assistant coach to Wenger who took three days to paint the first one. Holtz loved it and had many printed. He hung on the wall of a narrow staircase leading to the field.

He told his players, "Every time you hit this sign, I want you to remember all the great people that played here before you, all the sacrifices that your teammates have made for you, all the people, your coaches, your parents, who are responsible for you being here."

Notre Dame football still utilizes this sign and slogan. It's a good vision or goal for a football team. The story has a sweet, unknown twist to it. That slogan has been copyrighted and has made a lot of money. Notre Dame doesn't get it, though, Laurie Wenger does. "I have MS," says Wenger, who retired from Notre Dame in 2009 but still lives in South Bend. "So, it really helps pay my medical bills."[38]

38 Rick Reilly, "Paint Like A Champion," *ESPN.com*, https://www.espn.com/espn/story/_/id/8765862/notre-dame-play-champion-today-sign

"Play Like A Champion" works for Notre Dame. What is the vision for your ministry? What is it that will inspire your team? What will challenge them to remember who they are and how they got there? I don't know if you find a Laurie Wenger but do what you can to create a vision.

Summary

Getting volunteers, training them and inspiring them to be what God has created them to be isn't easy, but it is crucial for successful ministry. Be committed to Godly character, pray and seek out those God has put in your sphere. Bob Russell was the minister of Southeast Christian Church in Louisville, Kentucky. When he arrived at the church its attendance was under 200 people. When he retired, the church was seeing a weekly attendance of 19,000 people. It's a remarkable story of what God can do. Russell once said, "Are you willing to do something so big that if God isn't in it, it will fail?"[39] That's the question for us, too. Are you?

Questions for Reflection

1. As you search for and pray for volunteers to serve in your ministry, what are some characteristics you're looking for? What matters the most to you? Why?

2. What do you think makes people hesitant to volunteer or serve in ministries? What can you do to help them overcome those obstacles?

3. Why is it important to explain to volunteers what is expected of them? What is your best method of communication? How can you maximize that in communicating to those you work with?

4. Brainstorm some ways you might show your appreciation to volunteers. What is the most appealing to you?

---

39 "A Date with Katrina," https://www.qsl.net/w8wn/katrina/katrina.html

5. Identify a time when you were inspired to give more or do more. What were the conditions around that? What did the coach or teacher do? How did you and your teammates respond?

6. What do you think prevents leaders from having honest and hard conversations with volunteers? How can you overcome it?

Chapter 4

Organization

"Organizing provides the structure through which a group of persons committed to and involved in a common enterprise do their work."[40] One of the more frustrating aspects of ministry is the lack of organization or an unwieldy organizational structure. Poorly designed organizational structures lead to uncertainty among volunteers, confusion about responsibilities and ineffective accountability. Bob I. Johnson identifies the core of a Godly organizational structure. He writes, "To begin, one must start thinking about getting organized for creative and redemptive expressions of ministry."[41] Our goal needs to set up our ministry in the way that allows for the best and most creative ideas to flow and become reality so that our ministry objective is met. The Bible notes the importance of organization.

What the Bible Says About Organizing

Reading Genesis 1 shows us God's creativity. It leaps from the page as we see God move through the six days of creation. What may sometimes get overlooked, though, is his organizational prowess. "For God is not a God of disorder but of peace — as in all the congregations of the Lord's people" (1 Corinthians 14:33). The Bible speaks to the importance of organization.

1 Corinthians 14:40

But everything should be done in a fitting and orderly way.

---

40 Bob I. Johnson, "How to Organize and Coordinate," *Christian Education Handbook*, Bruce P. Powers, ed, B & H Publishers, Nashville, 1996, p. 60.

41 *Ibid*, p. 61

Proverbs 13:4

A sluggard's appetite is never filled, but the desires of the diligent are fully satisfied.

Luke 14:28-30

"Suppose one of you wants to build a tower. Won't you first sit down and estimate the cost to see if you have enough money to complete it? For if you lay the foundation and are not able to finish it, everyone who sees it will ridicule you, saying, 'This person began to build and wasn't able to finish.'

Acts 6:1-4

In those days when the number of disciples was increasing, the Hellenistic Jews among them complained against the Hebraic Jews because their widows were being overlooked in the daily distribution of food. So, the twelve gathered all the disciples together and said, "It would not be right for us to neglect the ministry of the word of God in order to wait on tables. Brothers and sisters choose seven men from among you who are known to be full of the Spirit and wisdom. We will turn this responsibility over to them and will give our attention to prayer and the ministry of the word."

Exodus 21:18-23

"But select capable men from all the people — men who fear God, trustworthy men who hate dishonest gain — and appoint them as officials over thousands, hundreds, fifties and tens. Have them serve as judges for the people at all times but have them bring every difficult case to you; the simple cases they can decide themselves. That will make your load lighter, because they will share it with you. If you do this and God so commands, you will be able to stand the strain, and all these people will go home satisfied."

What Do We Mean By "Organizational Structure?"

A basic definition of "organizational structure" is "a system used to define a hierarchy within an organization. It identifies each job, its function and where it reports to within the organization."[42] That's a lot of business jargon, what does that mean in simpler terms? It's the way the leader and volunteers work together, report to one another and accomplish the task of ministry. Here are some different models of ministry organization.

Four Different Organizational Structures

1. Functional — In this structure, there is a person to whom all the others report and are accountable. The work is then divided up among the volunteers with each one being assigned a part or aspect based on gifts, talents, training or ability.

   If we were to look at a functional structure for a children's ministry worship program for preteens, it might look like this. The children's minister would oversee the entire ministry and all in it would be accountable to her. She would place people under her to accomplish various aspects of the ministry. She might have someone to plan and do the singing and opening part of the worship time. She may have another person that would plan and implement the art or craft project each week. She might have a third person that sits with the students throughout the time and is responsible for monitoring behavior. She is over all of it but has delegated specific responsibilities to others. Each volunteer is responsible for only his/her part. It's functional in the sense that each person does what he/she is equipped to do under the direction of the leader.

---

42 "What is the meaning of organizational structure?" https://smallbusiness.chron.com/meaning-organizational-structure-3803.html

2. Divisional — This structure is an extension of a functional system but is more effective for a larger ministry. In this system, there is a leader at the top and the different ministry programs are led by volunteers below them. Under those volunteers are workers who, in a functional system, get the work done.

   Let's revisit the children's ministry and take a broader view. The children's minister oversees many different programs. She's got the Sunday morning program for preschool and elementary kids. She has a Wednesday night program for both groups, and she does Vacation Bible School. In a Divisional approach, she would have a person that would oversee Sunday morning preschool, Sunday morning elementary and so on. She would then oversee the leaders of each component of ministry. This doesn't excuse her from being involved. It simply divides large tasks into manageable sizes and responsibilities.

3. Project Driven — In this structure, there isn't as much formal set up. The principle here is that a group of people (the leader and volunteers) have a task to do. The group is selected and agree to work together. As they meet, there is not an identified leader as such. The group determines the best approach to complete the project and assigns different aspects of it by mutual agreement. The leader may have ultimate accountability for the project being finished, but the group isn't leader driven.

   Our children's minister may want to have a "Back to School" event. After prayer, she may select volunteers who share the same passion and dream. She will then bring the volunteers in. They will brainstorm, dream and allow a plan to emerge. Organically, the roles of the members is fleshed out and the project is started. Once the project is complete, so is the work of this group.

4. One Person Band — This structure is the least effective one. What happens to force this structure is that the leader is the only one who has the passion and vision for the ministry. He/she doesn't or is unable to inspire others to join them, so he/she does all the tasks to accomplish the goal.

In our children's minster example, it might be that the children's minister is passionate about doing a children's musical. She is unable or doesn't pass that dream on to other volunteer leaders, so she is leading it by herself. This happens in ministry from time to time but is never the best way to get things done.

These are four examples of organizational structure for ministry. It isn't an exhaustive list. Most ministries, though, use one of these or a hybrid to get the task done. There isn't a preferred one over another (except for the "one-person band" which is never the best choice). Which one you decided to use will be determined by many factors. Before deciding which structure you'll use to frame your ministry, consider some important principles.

Principles of Effective Organizational Structures

Doris Freese writes of organization that "it puts wheels under the program to get it moving."[43] Here are six principles that will help develop an effective organizational structure. Whatever organizational structure you choose, it needs to be...

1. Unified — The way your ministry is set up ought to bring about maximum effectiveness of each part to bring about the big goal of the ministry. The goal ought to be the emphasis throughout the facets of your organizational chart.

2. Simple — One of the big keys to a successful organizational system is that it's understandable and easy to be a part of. Too many times ministries can get bogged

---

43 Doris Freese, "Understanding and Using Curriculum," *Christian Education: Foundations for the Future*, ed. Robert E. Clark, Moody, 1991, p. 402

down and hindered by an organizational structure that is overly complicated or too awkward. Aim for having just enough structure to make a ministry solid but not weighed down by it.

3. Flexible — The structure you launch a ministry using may not be the most effective one in year number two. Don't make the organizational approach the master and the goal subservient to it. Use or adapt whatever approach works well for the current situation.

4. Cooperative — The organizational system you adopt needs to bring out the best in all those who work with you. It should promote a sense of team and working together. Sometimes the danger, especially of functional structures, is that they can foster a "lone ranger" mentality among your workers.

5. Engaging — The organizational structure you select for your ministry ought to appeal to those who work with you. It should provide enough support, so they don't feel isolated, on an island. It shouldn't be so heavy, though, that they feel burdened by it. It needs to be a structure that challenges your volunteers and pushes them to do their best.

6. Interpersonal — The structure you utilize for your ministry has to be centered on how people can work together to accomplish the ministry goal. It seems obvious, but every ministry involves people working with other people to develop or grow a personal relationship with Jesus. If your organizational structure inhibits people from working together, it probably isn't the best way to do it.

What are the Benefits of Having a Good Organizational Structure

Why does all this matter? Why not just let things play out as they do and not worry about it? Good organization is a part of what makes an endeavor successful. Benjamin Franklin once said, "For every minute spent organizing, an hour is earned."[44] Ministry can be exhausting and take a lot of time. If good organization can help better use that time and allow us to concentrate on other facets of ministry, why wouldn't we want to be organized? Here are some benefits that accrue from spending time making sure things are structured properly.

1. Quality organization enables volunteers to know what their roles are and clearly establishes an accountability system. Nothing is more frustrating working in a ministry than not knowing what you're supposed to do or what you are accountable for. Organization sets up a ministry for success.

2. Quality organization empowers people to accomplish the goal of the ministry. When everyone on the team knows what his/her role is and what he/she can and needs to do to accomplish it, ministry is authorized to do what needs to be done. Your volunteers know what they are able and expected to do in any given circumstance. When things happen, the ministry isn't paralyzed by those working in it wondering who is supposed to do something.

3. Quality organization allows the work of the ministry to be appropriately divided. It's easy, especially in ministry, to find the bulk of the work being done by a small number of people. Quality organization better divides the work and engages more volunteers in meaningful work.

4. Quality organization demonstrates how each function or part of a ministry works to support and enhance other parts. Working in something bigger than we are is important. A good organizational structure allows everyone in your ministry to see how what they are doing contributes to the success.

44 Benjamin Franklin, https://morethanorganized.net/time-productivity/

5. Quality organization emphasizes teamwork and involvement. If roles are established and worth is attached to each part of what's being done, a good team is created.

6. Quality organization allows for the ministry to grow, adapt and improve over time. If the organizational structure is too rigid, the ministry can't grow beyond its confines. If it is too loose, it will likely collapse with no support. Quality structure allows for growth and improvement.

How Do I Know What Organizational Structure Will Be the Best?

The next component in developing an effective organizational structure is to make the decision which approach will best suit your ministry. This comes down to a personal choice, but there are some things you ought to consider as you make this decision.

1. Pray — Noted in every chapter, this cannot be bypassed or ignored. Before selecting how a ministry is going to be set up, pray. Ask the Holy Spirit to lead you to design the ministry that God wants to accomplish this task.

2. Recognize that the nature of the work to be done will help determine the structure — Simply put, this is the awareness that what you're doing, in the practical sense, will help direct you to the best organizational structure. For example, if you are setting up an entire student ministry, you might not use a "functional" structure. It might make more sense to use a "Divisional" structure that will put a volunteer over each larger part of the ministry. If you are doing a lock-in for students, you might find the "project-driven" approach works better than a "functional" system and a lot better than a "one man band."

3. Allow decisions to be made as close to the ground as possible — Train, equip and trust your volunteers to make decisions about what is going on in the ministry as they work in the front lines of it. There must be accountability and responsibility attached to this, but a volunteer who must go back continually and ask a leader to accomplish basic things is not effective. This principle requires trust and needs to be continually evaluated, but the leader who has prepared and trusts his/her volunteers to implement the ministry and make decisions is an effective leader.

4. Don't Worship the Organizational Structure — There are times when we fall in love with the way we do things (as opposed to what we're doing.) This isn't helpful and we must guard against it. The structure is there to serve you, your volunteers and your people. It is there to facilitate your ministry goal. When the organizational structure inhibits any of these, it must be changed, no matter how much we like it.

5. Make communication a priority — We'll look closer at this a bit later, but in any effective organizational structure, communication is the fuel that makes it go. Adhere to the idea that you can never over-communicate.

Organization is about People

Gilbert Rhode, a home designer, once said in a meeting with colleagues, "The most crucial thing about a community of faith is the people who have been and will be touched by the love and grace of Jesus Christ."[45] It's important to remember, as we plan an organizational structure, that people are the most important part of what we're doing. We must keep in mind that while we may like working with numbers, spreadsheets and data, our number one thing is people.

45 Guy Sayles, "What's the Most Important Part of Church?" *EthicsDaily.com*, https://ethicsdaily.com/whats-the-most-important-part-of-church-cms-19886/ August 10, 2012.

Keeping in mind that people are most important, there are some important things that we ought to consider as we select an organizational structure.

1. The structure we utilize must not prohibit or inhibit work being done by the volunteers in your ministry.

   It's possible to set up an organizational structure that hinders rather than helps volunteers accomplish ministry. Consider the plight of today's public-school teachers. Many feel burdened and held captive to enormous amounts of paperwork that keep them from interacting with and teaching kids. Holly Ashton used to be a teacher. She said, "I love working with the kids. The amount of paperwork I had to do (as a teacher) was really cumbersome. It took me away from the kids."[46]

   The public schools are battling an organizational structure that may be preventing the workers from accomplishing what is the primary goal of schools; teaching kids. We must make sure that we don't set up a structure that inhibits us in accomplishing ministry.

2. The structure we utilize must be enable us to teach, grow, inspire and challenge people. They are the "product," if you will.

   Sometimes the result of what we're wanting to accomplish gets lost in the process of doing it. I know that sounds crazy, but we can get so caught up in *how* we're doing what we're doing that we forget the *what* of what we're doing. In Mark Twain's novel, *The Adventures of Huckleberry Finn*, there is a scene in chapter 34 in which Tom and Huck help Jim escape from a small, farm cabin he's being held in and lead him to freedom. He could be set free by simply removing a board and Huck is for that. However, Tom

---

46 Dan Benson, and Julie Grace, "Teachers want to help kids, not do paperwork," Badger Institute, January 25, 2018. https://www.badgerinstitute.org/News/2017-2018/Teachers-want-to-help-kids-not-do-paperwork.htm

Sawyer isn't. He argues that the plan is not complicated enough and then decides that they should dig Jim out because doing so will take a couple of weeks. Tom Sawyer isn't for doing anything unless it's done properly.

That's a ridiculous situation and it's supposed to be. It's foolish to get so wrapped up in how we do something that we forget what's important, doing it.

Why are people so important? They were important to Jesus. Matthew 12:18-22 quotes from Isaiah 42.

> *"Here is my servant whom I have chosen,*
> *the one I love, in whom I delight;*
> *I will put my Spirit on him,*
> *and he will proclaim justice to the nations.*
> *He will not quarrel or cry out;*
> *no one will hear his voice in the streets.*
> *A bruised reed he will not break,*
> *and a smoldering wick he will not snuff out,*
> *till he has brought justice through to victory.*
> *In his name the nations will put their hope."*

People mattered to Jesus. He had time for people who were outcasts, like the woman with the bleeding problem. He spoke to people who were rascals, like Zacchaeus the tax collector. He touched the untouchable, like the leprous man who came to him for help. Jesus was about people. If our ministries are to be like Jesus, we must be about people, too.

Communication: What Makes Organization Go

As we noted earlier in this chapter, communication is the fuel that makes the organization go. The ability to communicate is vital to the success of any ministry. Establishing lines of communication and allowing them to function well early in your ministry is crucial for success. Failure to communicate is usually disastrous. Here are some general guidelines that can help you foster good communication.

First, establish open channels throughout your ministry. Make sure that your volunteers know that they can come to you at any time. It's also important that you visit regularly with your people. Don't wait until there is a problem or issue before you talk to them. Engage with them often and make sure they know that your door is open to them.

Second, articulate plainly and often what your ministry goals are and what the plan is to accomplish that goal. You can't assume that everyone knows what's in your mind. You can't assume that if you've said it once, everyone got it. State the goals and the plan plainly, often and in multiple settings.

Third, plan regular times when you meet with and/or communicate with your volunteers. No one is overly fond of meetings. We have meetings a lot in the church. Meetings can spread like weeds on our daily planner. However, regular and consistent meetings are important if they are vehicles for communication and generation of ideas. In our culture today, we don't have to necessarily have face to face meetings. Technology allows for many different ways to meet with, connect with or communicate with volunteers. The bottom line is use it. Whether it is texts, face to face, email, or another method, make sure you share with those in your ministry.

Finally, communicate to everyone in your ministry. This doesn't mean you communicate everything to everyone, but it does mean that you have a line of communication with everyone who serves with you in ministry. It's frustrating for volunteers to feel "out of the loop." No one wants to have an "inner circle" and an "outer loop" in a ministry. While not everyone can or should know everything, make sure that everyone feels respected enough to be in the communication chain.

Before we leave the realm of communication, let's look at some things to avoid regarding sharing information.

First, make it a principle to not share "bad news" in an impersonal way (email or text). If you have to deal with a problem; if you have to ask someone to seek a different area of service; if you have to question a volunteer about what may have happened; do it **in person**. Talk with the person, face to face. It may be more difficult or awkward, but doing it face to face allows you to utilize all means of communication, verbal and non-verbal. It allows you to gain immediate feedback and it is biblical (Matthew 19).

Second, don't put off dealing with "bad news" thinking it will go away. It usually doesn't. This doesn't mean we don't pray when something comes up that requires our attention. It doesn't mean that we don't seek wise counsel before acting. It does, though, mean that after our due diligence, we act. Whether we have to have a one to one meeting or share bad news with a group, don't put it off, hoping it will go away.

Third, when you find yourself in a tense situation and the communication is tough, work hard to respond and not react. Responding is allowing the Holy Spirit to guide your words in a manner that is "always with grace, seasoned with salt" (Colossians 4:6). Reacting is when we allow our emotions to take control and we react with anger, hurt, betrayal and a host of other non-helpful things.

Finally, understand that you are communicating with different people who have different personalities and communication skills and styles. Be flexible in your approach. Some people are tech savvy and utilize the latest technology with ease. Some of your volunteers, especially your older ones, may not be on social media. It's a simple point, but just be sure that you reach out to your people, all of them, in ways in which they are comfortable and fluent.

What Organization Says About your Ministry

Before we end this chapter, let's look at what organization says about your ministry. People look at and judge a ministry, often, on how it appears to them. What they're often seeing is the skeleton structure of how it looks. How we set up our ministries reveals something about what we value. Consider these principles.

1. Our organizational structure reveals what we value and what our goal is. These things are evident in an effective organizational structure. When people see that our structure allows for people to engage with

people, they conclude people matter. When the system allows for people to bring about the goal, they can identify that this ministry is about this goal. A good check on how effectively your structure is working is to ask those with whom you work to identify what they believe matters in your ministry. If the structure is solid, the goals and people will dominate their answers.

2. Our organizational structure demonstrates that we accept accountability and responsibility. An effective organizational structure has accountability and responsibility (financial, spiritual and practical). No matter what we do in ministry, we have to uphold the highest standard of biblical accountability.

3. Our organizational structure, if effective, promotes our mission to those around us. Our structure can help those in the broader church family to understand the mission of our ministry. It can also generate excitement and enthusiasm for our ministry. A ministry that is poorly organized or doesn't function well communicates to the church at large that our ministry doesn't matter. Hardly anyone gets excited about something that seems like a mess.

4. Our organizational structure, if appropriate, invites participation among those who might be served by the ministry and those who might serve in it. People tend to want to be a part of things that are going well. How they see your ministry as they view your structure can be inviting.

Though organization can be tough, it speaks volumes about what we believe and how dedicated we are to our mission.

Summary

Organization is a critical and, many times, overlooked part of ministry. It isn't as fun as perhaps some other components. It certainly isn't a glamourous part. It does matter.

Edmund Burke once said, "Good order is the foundation of all things."[47] Prayerfully organize your ministry for success.

Questions for Reflection

1. Why does it seem to be hard to organize ministry effectively? What are the barriers to organizing a ministry to get the maximum result? Why do you think an organizational structure matters? How do you see it helping a ministry?

2. What do the Bible passages tell us about how God is organized? Do you think of God in that way? Why or why not?

3. Of the four different organizational models suggested in this chapter, which one have you seen in operation the most? Which one the least? What are some strengths and weaknesses that you see in each one?

4. What benefits do you see coming from being organized well? How important is it to evaluate your organizational structure?

5. How would you describe the process of selecting the best organizational system for your ministry? What might make that hard for you?

6. In your opinion, what are the best ways to communicate with those in your ministry? Why is communication so difficult? How would a good communication system assist your ministry? What are some bad things that happen when people don't communicate well?

7. People were Jesus' business and they are ours. How is your ministry doing emphasizing people? In what ways can you improve? Why does emphasizing people matter?

8. Why is it hard to communicate "bad things?" Why is it important we do it?

47 Edmund Burke, https://www.theorderexpert.com/11-inspirational-quotes-about-organization/

Chapter 5

Curriculum

Selecting what to study and learn is important. There are some who simply say, "We're just going to teach the Bible." There's nothing wrong with that, in fact, there's a lot right with it. The question is, though, how do you do that? That's where curriculum comes into the picture. "Good curriculum is designed to facilitate Bible teaching, not replace it. Therefore, an understanding of what curriculum is and how to choose and use it effectively is essential for Christian education."[48]

Obtaining, creating, adapting and evaluating what you teach is vital to success in any educational ministry of the church. What is taught matters and there's a biblical imperative that demands we be true to God's word. How do we do that? What are some practical principles that I can use in my ministry? How would I attempt to write or adapt curriculum? All these are important discussion points and we'll address them. Let's begin with the biblical caution regarding what we teach.

What the Bible Says About Teaching and What We Teach

The Bible makes it clear that what we teach and pass on to others matters. Teachers will be held accountable for what they tell others. It is important that we commit to teach the things of God in a way that is relevant, engaging and meaningful. Here are some scriptures that help us understand the importance of what we teach and teaching itself.

James 3:1-2

Not many of you should become teachers, my fellow believers, because you know that we who teach will be judged more strictly.

---

48 Lin Johnson, "Understanding and Using Curriculum," *Christian Education: Foundations for the Future*, ed. Robert E. Clark, Moody, 1991, p. 495.

We all stumble in many ways. Anyone who is never at fault in what they say is perfect, able to keep their whole body in check.

Titus 2:7-8

In everything set them an example by doing what is good. In your teaching show integrity, seriousness and soundness of speech that cannot be condemned, so that those who oppose you may be ashamed because they have nothing bad to say about us.

Proverbs 22:6

Start children off on the way they should go, and even when they are old they will not turn from it.

2 Timothy 3:16-17

All Scripture is God-breathed and is useful for teaching, rebuking, correcting and training in righteousness, so that the servant of God may be thoroughly equipped for every good work.

Deuteronomy 4:8-10

And what other nation is so great as to have such righteous decrees and laws as this body of laws I am setting before you today? Only be careful and watch yourselves closely so that you do not forget the things your eyes have seen or let them fade from your heart as long as you live. Teach them to your children and to their children after them. Remember the day you stood before the Lord your God at Horeb, when he said to me, "Assemble the people before me to hear my words so that they may learn to revere me as long as they live in the land and may teach them to their children."

Principles for Choosing an Appropriate Curriculum

Selecting a quality curriculum requires diligence and discernment. How do I find good material? What are the things I should note as I choose? Here are some important principles to consider?

We start with the big picture in mind.

1. As you begin to evaluate curriculum, ask yourself which ones fit or are compatible with my theological understanding?

   It's important to address this at the beginning. There are lots of publishers that produce teaching material for the church. There are, as you already know, lots of different churches, too. I adhere to an adage in the Restoration Movement (Christian Churches/Churches of Christ) of which I am a member. It says, "We're Christians only, but not the only Christians."[49] Though that's true, it doesn't mean that all who wear the name of Jesus agree on everything. As you begin to select a Sunday school curriculum or a teaching plan for your student ministry, it will always be wise to assess the theological content. Does it line up with the teachings of the church as a whole? Are there parts that might need to be modified a bit to be acceptable?

   Also check for the version of the Bible the curriculum or lessons utilize. I don't know that this is a huge deal for most teaching material, but you ought to know the preferred version. There are some churches that have a version that they require. You'll want to know that as you select a curriculum.

   The evaluation that's called for here is for more than just the subtle theological differences between two branches of protestant teaching, though that is important. In our current culture there's a lot of material published that portrays Jesus and salvation in unscriptural ways. You'll never be wrong to thoroughly investigate what you are teaching or allowing others to teach people in your ministry.

2. Next, check on content consistency. You may be wanting a Sunday school program in which the lessons for one age group feed into the next age group and down the line. In education circles this is called the Scope

---

49 "Key Principles of the Restoration Movement," http://www.eccnorthamerica.com/key-principles-of-the-restoration-movement.html

and Sequence. It may be that you desire, for your student ministry, the boys to study or discuss one thing and the girls another. Does the curriculum you've selected allow for this?

Another facet to consider, under the umbrella of content consistency, is does the curriculum anchor to the Bible in a way that you find appropriate? Not every curriculum utilizes the Bible in the same way. You'll need to consider what you think is correct for your situation and make sure the material you use meets that standard.

3. Then, once you've considered these two things, you'll need to think about what it is that your group needs. What is it that God wants to share with your people?

It shouldn't surprise you that I suggest you begin to address this question by first praying. Seek what the Holy Spirit puts on your heart regarding what your people need. Once you've sought the Holy Spirit's direction, allow what he says to guide your search.

You'll then want to consider your church's unique situation. For what age groups are you planning to use this curriculum? How long is the teaching time for this particular component of your ministry? Which of the materials you're looking at best presents the material you are convinced your people need to know or hear? Maybe you have a very active group or maybe you have one that is more into a video presentation? Which of the curriculum plans you're examining is the best fit for your group?

These questions are important and can't be overlooked. Let's be honest. There is a lot of quality stuff out there. The choice of what to use isn't often between what is terrible and what is good. It often comes down to what best fits our needs. That's what these questions determine. This process will likely bring the potential choices down to three or four options. What's next?

Once we have the big picture in mind, narrow down the focus by examining the specific questions relevant to your ministry. Regarding the material you're looking at...

1. Does it work well with the size of your group? This is a simple question, but important. If the curriculum calls for a lot of breakout groups and your whole group is the size of a breakout group, that may not be the most effective for you. If the curriculum calls for a lot of back and forth discussion and you have a large group, that won't work for you. Evaluate if the format of the material is workable for you.

2. What are the media requirements for the material and does your church have them? If the curriculum requires overhead projectors and video, do you have them? If it requires internet access, do you have it? Does it work effectively? Does the material require each participant to have anything specific? If so, can you get that, too? Is that something that your group will engage with?

3. Does the material account for special-needs participants? This may or may not affect your group now, but it is something that ought to be considered. We want to and ought to be able to minister to all kids, so asking this question early in the process can be helpful.

4. Is the material reproducible? Is it okay to make copies of parts of it or is it copyrighted? How easy is the material to get to each person in your group? Much of the material produced today allows for a certain number of copies to be made. Some, though, require that each participant purchase the material. This is something you need to know. It's wrong to make copies of copyrighted material.

5. Is the material easy to understand? This applies to both those hearing/learning it and those who might have to teach it. Is it structured in a simple manner?

Does it have all the leader might need at his/her fingertips or does it require a lot of work at home to get a lesson ready? The answers to these questions might help you decide between two fine options.

6. Is the material print or online? If it is online, is it downloadable? There's lots of good material online and many publishers are utilizing the download option. That may or may not work for you. It's worth considering.

7. How much does it cost? This is a practical, real question that all in ministry have to address. Budget concerns are real. Hardly anyone in ministry can buy whatever he/she wants. You may have to decide how much of your budget goes into purchasing teaching materials. If so, this question is important.

What About Writing Your Own?

There are lots of good teaching materials that engage students with the Bible and help them encounter Jesus Christ. If you follow the steps mentioned earlier in this chapter, it won't be hard to find one that suits your needs. However, for some, there is a benefit to writing you own curriculum. If that's what you find yourself drawn to, how do you go about doing it?

First, pray and see what the Lord would have you do. It may be that you need to do a study for which there isn't a published curriculum. Even if you've already ascertained that, pray as you write. May the Holy Spirit guide your mind and your words as you create the lessons.

Next, read and study the Bible passages you are using for the study. Use good commentary to gain an understanding of background, word use and concepts. There isn't a shortcut, especially if you're writing your own material, around studying and knowing what the text says.

Once you have an idea of the text, you're ready to outline the lesson or lesson series. Organize the main points of the passage and target them as the lesson aims. If you are doing an entire series of lessons, at this point you may be listing the different topics each lesson will cover. For an individual lesson or each lesson in a series, develop the main points (what it is that this passage is telling those who are studying it). These main teaching points are the skeleton upon which your lesson hangs.

After you've studied, understand the text and can articulate the main points, you'll need to create the presentation. As you do this, flesh out what comes under each main point. This is the body of the lesson. In this part of the process, you'll need to figure out the kind of presentation this will be. Will you utilize discussion? If so, write it that way. Will there be a media or technology component? If so, this is the time to plan for that. How and if a craft project or game fits in is addressed as you work out what the lesson looks like.

Once that stage is finished, examine how you will launch this lesson and how you will land it. The introduction is important. It's in the introduction that people hear why this lesson matters. The introduction, if done well, piques interest and curiosity. It also grabs the hearer in such a way that he or she wants to know more. Creativity and humor often lead to memorable introductions.

Once you've launched the lesson and taught it, you must land it. This is the most important part. How do you conclude? It comes down to what do you believe Jesus, through the text, is challenging your people to do? The landing is where you give the application. Ask yourself the following questions that your students may have for you as you prepare the conclusion.

1. How does this affect my life?
2. What specific things should I do with what you've just told me?
3. What difference does any of this make?
4. How does what you've just told me make me more like Jesus?
5. So what?

There are both benefits and drawbacks to writing your own lessons. The benefits include a more direct, prayer guided selection of text and material that your people need. It also allows you to approach the material in a more flexible manner as you write it to fit your own needs. The drawbacks include having to do significantly more research and work. You'll have to create your own extra materials or adapt them from another curriculum.

As you approach the issue of curriculum, there are many great places where you can get curriculum and you should check them out. It's also possible that, for a season, the best thing is for you to write your own. If you are uncertain about what material is out there, get online and use a search engine; visit your nearby Christian bookstore or look through a catalog of materials. Quality curriculum is important.

Areas of Different Curriculum

Before we move to the next phase of curriculum, it's important to realize that there are lots of programming in the church that uses curriculum. Here is a brief overview of the different areas of ministry and the types of curriculum they might need.

1. Adult Ministries
    If you are overseeing adult ministries, you'll need to consider some or possibly all the following areas regarding curriculum...
    A. Sunday school classes
    B. Life groups or small groups
    C. Bible studies
    D. Discipleship groups
    E. Men's ministry
    F. Women's ministry

If this is your area, you'll want to consider the different components of each of these ministries and what their mission is in relation to that of the whole church. Your choice of curriculum for each one should follow the principles outlined above.

2. Children's Ministry
   If you are tasked with the children's ministry, some or all these areas will need to have some curriculum...
   A. Sunday school for preschool through elementary school.
   B. Kids' worship or kids' church for the whole range of ages.
   C. Wednesday night program for preschool through elementary school.
   D. Vacation Bible School for kids through elementary school.
   E. Bible clubs for all ages of kids.

If this is your area, you'll want to analyze what the needs of each group is in connection with the purpose and mission. Children's ministry often involves at least two different "loops" of curriculum. You must have one curriculum for your preschool kids and at least one more for your elementary kids. Sometimes you can find one curriculum that covers all of them, but not always.

3. Student Ministry
   If your ministry is for students or youths, then you have to make some choices, too.
   A. What you do for your large group lesson is important. It may connect with your breakout groups as well.
   B. You also might have a Sunday morning or a Sunday school choice to make for your students.
   C. Student life groups — It might be that you have student life groups. If so, they will need material, too.

If this is your area, you will have to familiarize yourself with curriculum choices and consider how you can best communicate and what you want to communicate to your students.

Evaluating How Well a Curriculum is Doing

Once we have a curriculum in place, we need to check for its effectiveness. We've addressed earlier why evaluation is important. Evaluating our curriculum is essential to ensuring that we're doing the best we can to teach eternal truths in a real, practical manner. Here are some guidelines that can assist you in making sure what you teach and how you're teaching it is effective. Once you've done the program for a portion of time (two or three months minimum)…

1. Listen to what your people say about it and compare that to the mission and goals that you have for the group. Listening to those in your group is important and often overlooked. The comments of your people should help you determine if you are communicating the purpose or mission of your group. It will also help you determine if this curriculum is accomplishing that task.

2. Honestly create a list of strengths and weaknesses. You can do this on your own, but it is better to get your leaders/volunteers together to create this list. What are some of the positive things you've seen in the last three months? What are some positive comments from those in the group? What are some things you wish you could have/would have done better? What things just didn't work? Don't be afraid to honestly confront these issues and encourage your leaders/volunteers to talk openly.

3. Sit down with your group of volunteers/leaders and make sure that what you are doing in the group is lining up with the purpose of the ministry as a whole. Does the curriculum point the people where you want them to look? Does the material make them think about things that matter in the big picture?

4. Sit down with your group of volunteers/leaders and assess if the curriculum is being understood well and taught in the best manner. It may be that the material is fine, but the way you have chosen to present it is hindering its effectiveness.

5. Discuss with your group of volunteers/leaders if the material is cost-effective. This is simply the question, "Are you getting enough bang for your buck?"

It's important to regularly and consistently evaluate what we're teaching and how we've chosen to teach it. Doing so will only improve your ministry.

Summary

The choice of what to teach in a ministry setting is significant. It isn't something that should be done lightly. Teaching about Jesus matters greatly and there's a lot of responsibility and accountability attached to it. Prayerfully consider the needs of your group and what you believe Jesus wants them/needs them to know. Do a diligent and thorough search of what is out there and what might best fit your needs. Consider, perhaps, writing your own. Once you have the material in place, don't settle. Continue to evaluate and ask yourself, "How can we do better?"

Questions for Reflection

1. In your opinion, why does what we teach about God, Jesus, the Holy Spirit and the Bible matter? Why is it something to take so seriously?

2. How would you respond to someone who might say, "I don't really need Christian teaching. It isn't really important."

3. What are some of the more difficult challenges of finding a good curriculum? What are some things you can do to make that task a bit easier?

4. The chapter asks you to consider the spiritual needs of those you work with. Prayer is essential in that process. What are some other things you can do to know what the needs of your people are?

5. What do you see are some advantages of creating your own curriculum? What would you see as some disadvantages?

6. The chapter lists several things to consider as you select a curriculum. Thinking of your own ministry (or a future one), which of these things do you consider the most important? Which of them, in your opinion, is least important? Why?

7. Evaluating curriculum is important, but it is often overlooked. Why do you think that's the case? Do you think many ministries strive to do better and ask themselves the hard questions? Why or why not?

Chapter 6

Why the Bible Matters

In Christian education there is nothing more important than the Bible. The Bible is God's revealed message to us and is at the heart of what we do and teach. "The core of the Christian faith is the confidence that our Creator God is, that he has acted in Christ Jesus to redeem, and that he has revealed himself and truth to us in his written word." [50]

It seems like making the Bible the focal point of Christian teaching is a "no-brainer," but there is some discussion. Matt Idom wrote, "God is the author of grace, not the Bible."[51] Andy Stanley said, in a 2018 message, ""I think [some people] put [the Bible] in the place of Jesus."[52] These comments are certainly debatable. For our purpose, we recognize while we don't worship the Bible, we do exalt the scriptures above any other book or teaching. It is the inerrant, authoritative Word of God. All of these descriptions matter.

It is inerrant. As it was originally penned by the author it is without error or mistake. This is important. We can rely on the Bible to be true and accurate.

It is authoritative. The Bible speaks to issues of life and human relationships in a way that is right and true. Because of what it is and whose it is, it occupies a position to speak truth.

It is the Word of God. The Bible comes from God. His Holy Spirit breathed the message into the hearts and minds of human writers. The Bible is God's message to fallen humanity.

We recognize the Bible is what points us to Jesus and reveals for us God's love and his redemptive plan for humanity.

---

50 Lawrence O. Richards, *Christian Education: Seeking to Become Like Jesus*, Zondervan, Grand Rapids, 1975, p. 309.

51 Matt Idom, "Worshipping God, Not the Bible," *Huffington Post*, May 25, 2011

52 Jason Daye, "Andy Stanley: Why I Stopped Saying 'The Bible Says' When I Preach," September 19, 2018, https://churchleaders.com/podcast/333806-andy-stanley-bible-inerrancy-evangelism.html

It isn't the object of our worship. It is, however, the foundation of what we believe and God's revelation for all humanity. Studying, teaching and knowing the Bible matters.

What does the Bible Say?

We'll begin by looking at the claims the Bible makes for itself. We recognize the authority of Scripture and not what it claims for itself.

2 Timothy 3:16-17

All Scripture is God-breathed and is useful for teaching, rebuking, correcting and training in righteousness, so that the servant of God may be thoroughly equipped for every good work.

2 Kings 17:13-14

The Lord warned Israel and Judah through all his prophets and seers: "Turn from your evil ways. Observe my commands and decrees, in accordance with the entire law that I commanded your ancestors to obey and that I delivered to you through my servants the prophets." But they would not listen and were as stiff-necked as their ancestors, who did not trust in the Lord their God.

Hebrews 1:1-2

In the past God spoke to our ancestors through the prophets at many times and in various ways, but in these last days he has spoken to us by his Son, whom he appointed heir of all things, and through whom also he made the universe.

2 Peter 1:20-21

Above all, you must understand that no prophecy of Scripture came about by the prophet's own interpretation of things. For prophecy never had its origin in the human will, but prophets, though human, spoke from God as they were carried along by the Holy Spirit.

Historical Evidence of the Truth of the Bible

This isn't an apologetics book, but I think it is important for us to acknowledge that the Bible is trustworthy. The key-word in this discussion is inerrant. The word "inerrant" means "without error."[53] Those of us who are in the evangelical camp of the Christian faith hold to the inerrancy of scripture. We believe the Bible to be, in its original manuscripts, without error.

If the Bible is at the center of what we teach and we claim it to be inerrant, how do we know? Again, there's a full study of this subject, but for our purposes here, let's summarize. Here are three observations that demonstrate why we can depend on the Bible.

First, the **text of the Bible is incredibly consistent**. Dr. Jason Lisle, director for Answers in Genesis and the Creation Museum, notes, "Another argument for the truthfulness of the Bible concerns its uniqueness and internal consistency. The Bible is remarkably self-consistent, despite having been written by more than forty different writers over a timespan of about 2,000 years. God's moral law, man's rebellion against God's law, and God's plan of salvation are the continuing themes throughout the pages of scripture. This internal consistency is what we would expect if the Bible really is what it claims to be — God's revelation."[54]

The Bible shows remarkable consistency which cannot be attributed to one human author, one time period or one setting. It doesn't contradict itself, nor does it vary or alter its themes. The consistency points to the ultimate author God. It is God's message, complete and unified, for all people always.

Second, we look to **archaeological discoveries**. The statement "Archeology cannot prove the Bible" is true. Archeology has, though, provided exciting and dramatic confirmation of the Bible's accuracy. Here are some examples:

1. Luke's account of events surrounding the birth of Je-

---

53 *Merriam-Webster Dictionary*, https://www.merriam-webster.com/dictionary/inerrant

54 Dr. Jason Lisle, "How Do We Know that the Bible Is True? Apologetics," March 22, 2011, https://answersingenesis.org/is-the-bible-true/how-do-we-know-that-the-bible-is-true/

sus — It's been suggested Luke erred regarding the events surrounding the birth of Jesus (Luke 2:1-3). Critics stated there was no census, Quirinius was not governor of Syria at that time, and everyone did not have to return to his ancestral home. Archeological discoveries, however, show that the Romans had a regular enrollment of taxpayers and held a census every fourteen years. This procedure began under Augustus. Discoveries also show Quirinius was, indeed, governor of Syria around 7 BC. It is supposed that he was governor twice, once in 7 BC and again in AD 6 (the date ascribed by Josephus.) A papyrus found in Egypt gives directions for the conduct of a census.[55]

2. The discovery of the ancient kingdom of Edom — New research claiming that the biblical kingdom of Edom was much older than scholars previously thought is demonstrating that the biblical record is trustworthy. The kingdom of Edom, long thought by many scholars to be in place long after Israel, has been shown to exist even before the formation of ancient Israel — just like it says in Genesis.[56]

3. Hezekiah's Siloam Tunnel Inscription — King Hezekiah of Judah ruled from 721 to 686 BC. Fearing a siege by the Assyrian king, Sennacherib, Hezekiah preserved Jerusalem's water supply by cutting a tunnel through 1,750 feet of solid rock from the Gihon Spring to the Pool of Siloam inside the city walls (2 Kings 20; 2 Chron. 32). At the Siloam end of the tunnel, an inscription, presently in the archaeological museum at Istanbul, Turkey, celebrates this remarkable accomplishment. The tunnel is probably the only biblical site that has not changed its appearance in

55 Sherri Bell, "Archeology Helps to Confirm the Historicity of the Bible," January 31, 2018, https://www.josh.org/archeology-validates-bible/

56 Ariel David, "Archaeology Confirms Book of Genesis on Israel's Arch-nemesis, the Edomites," Haaretz, September 18, 2019, https://www.haaretz.com/archaeology/. premium.MAGAZINE-archaeology-confirms-book-of-genesis-on-israel-s-arch-nemesis-the-edomites-1.7855111

2,700 years.[57]

These are simply three of what could be many examples. However, it is important to acknowledge that these do not prove the Bible to be true. They demonstrate that the Bible can be trusted and has proven to be by recent discoveries.

Third, the sheer number of **fulfilled prophecies** support the reliability of the Bible. There are over a hundred prophecies in the Old Testament that predict events that would happen in the life of Jesus, the Messiah, hundreds of years before they happened. The odds of one person being able to fulfill all these prophecies with one hundred percent accuracy, is 10 to the 18th power. In Daniel 2, God, in Nebuchadnezzar's dream, foretold of four world kingdoms, Babylon, Persia, Greece and Rome. [58] The sheer number of fulfilled prophecies speak to the inspired nature of the Word of God.

In conclusion, I like what Dr. Lisle writes:

The truth of the Bible is obvious to anyone willing to fairly investigate it. The Bible is uniquely self-consistent and extraordinarily authentic. It has changed the lives of millions of people who have placed their faith in Christ. It has been confirmed countless times by archaeology and other sciences. It possesses divine insight into the nature of the universe and has made correct predictions about distant future events with perfect accuracy. When Christians read the Bible, they cannot help but recognize the voice of their Creator. The Bible claims to be the Word of God, and it demonstrates this claim by making knowledge possible. It is the standard of standards.[59]

Why the Bible is at the Heart of What We Teach

It's hard to imagine a football team who never put on the pads. It would make no sense for a baseball team to attempt to play the national pastime without a bat and ball. These ideas are silly. No one would think of doing them. How crazy

---

57 Paul L. Maier, "Biblical Archaeology: Factual Evidence to Support the Historicity of the Bible," March 30, 2009, https://www.equip.org/article/biblical-archaeology-factual-evidence-to-support-the-historicity-of-the-bible/

58 "Is the Bible True," https://www.bibleinfo.com/en/questions/is-bible-true

59 Lisle, *Ibid.*

then, is it, to show people how to live and be more like Jesus and never use a Bible? I hear what you're saying; "that's dumb." I agree, but getting kids in the Bible isn't an easy task. A 2015 survey in England noted that fifty percent of young people who identify as Christians don't read their Bible more than once a month.[60] I think the problem is real across the Atlantic as well. Why is it important, especially for children's ministry workers and student ministry workers, to emphasize the Bible?

Here are some reasons.

1. It's through the Bible that I encounter God and Jesus in an objective way — God's character, passions and nature are revealed to us in Scripture. The Bible portrays for us in powerful ways who Jesus is and what he's done. Consider the following about God...

1 Corinthians 10:13
No temptation has overtaken you except what is common to mankind. And God is faithful; he will not let you be tempted beyond what you can bear. But when you are tempted, he will also provide a way out so that you can endure it.

1 John 1:5
This is the message we have heard from him and declare to you: God is light; in him there is no darkness at all.

James 1:17
Every good and perfect gift is from above, coming down from the Father of the heavenly lights, who does not change like shifting shadows.

John 4:24
God is spirit, and his worshipers must worship in the Spirit and in truth."

---

60 Marcus Jones, "Half of Christian teenagers don't read Bible more than once a month," July 22, 2015, https://www.premier.org.uk/News/UK/Half-of-Christian-teenagers-don-t-read-Bible-more-than-once-a-month?+news+23+july+Christian+Media

Here's what the Bible says about Jesus...

John 14:6
Jesus answered, "I am the way and the truth and the life. No one comes to the Father except through me.

1 Timothy 2:5
For there is one God and one mediator between God and mankind, the man Christ Jesus

Hebrews 13:8
Jesus Christ is the same yesterday and today and forever.

Philippians 2:8-11
And being found in appearance as a man, he humbled himself by becoming obedient to death — even death on a cross! Therefore God exalted him to the highest place and gave him the name that is above every name, that at the name of Jesus every knee should bow, in heaven and on earth and under the earth, and every tongue acknowledge that Jesus Christ is Lord, to the glory of God the Father.

2. The Bible gives me a standard of what is right, wrong, moral, immoral, and just — In a world where the lines between right and wrong are often blurred and absolute truth is rarely acknowledged, the Bible stands as a beacon of light and truth. David writes in Psalm 119:105, "Your word is a lamp for my feet, a light on my path." Proverbs 14:12 says, "There is a way that appears to be right, but in the end it leads to death."

   Elisabeth Elliot once said, "The Word of God I think of as a straight edge, which shows up our own crookedness. We can't really tell how crooked our thinking is until we line it up with the straight edge of Scripture."[61]

---

61 "25 Quotes from Influential Christians about the Bible," November 29, 2016, https://www.crosswalk.com/faith/spiritual-life/inspiring-quotes/25-quotes-from-influential-christians-about-the-bible.html

3. The Bible equips and empowers me to serve — It's through the encouragement and challenge of God's Word that I can be inspired to whatever I can for his kingdom. Consider Apollos. Acts 18:25-26 tells us about him and how instruction motivated him to even greater service. "He had been instructed in the way of the Lord, and he spoke with great fervor and taught about Jesus accurately, though he knew only the baptism of John. He began to speak boldly in the synagogue. When Priscilla and Aquila heard him, they invited him to their home and explained to him the way of God more adequately."

   Apollos became of even greater service for Jesus' kingdom after he'd been instructed by Priscilla and Aquila. 2 Timothy 3:16-17 also addresses this. "All Scripture is God-breathed and is useful for teaching, rebuking, correcting and training in righteousness, so that the servant of God[a] may be thoroughly equipped for every good work." 2 Timothy 2:15 also notes the importance of learning and being able to use God's Word. "Do your best to present yourself to God as one approved, a worker who does not need to be ashamed and who correctly handles the word of truth."

4. The Bible deepens my relationship with God, Jesus and the Holy Spirit — The more I learn and know about God, Jesus and the Holy Spirit, the more I'm drawn to them. Once I begin to fathom the incredible love God has for me; the amazing sacrifice Jesus made for me; and the abiding presence of the Holy Spirit in my life, I am compelled to yield more of me.

   Colossians 2:6 says, "So then, just as you received Christ Jesus as Lord, continue to live your lives in him."

   Matthew 11:28-30 records Jesus' words, "Come to me, all you who are weary and burdened, and I will give you rest. Take my yoke upon you and learn from me, for I am gentle and humble in heart, and you will find rest for your souls. For my yoke is easy and my burden is light."

As a carpenter needs a hammer; as a surgeon needs a scalpel, as a pilot needs a plane; Christians need the Bible.

What Bible Do I Use for My Group?

We've established that the Bible matters and is indispensable for Christian teaching. The question then becomes, "Which one do I use?" There are lots of different translations, which is the best? That is a subjective question, but it might be helpful to get an overview of the different major translations so you can choose wisely for your group.

There are quite a few differences among the various versions of the Bible available today. We'll start with some key principles to keep in mind.

1. There is a difference between a translation and a paraphrase.

   The difference between a translation and a paraphrase is straightforward. A translation is taking the text from one language to another language. So, going from Hebrew to English is a translation. However, a paraphrase involves starting and staying with the same language. To paraphrase means to restate the meaning of a text using different words in the same language.

   Within the framework of a translation, there are different kinds. For English Bibles, there are two dominant translation methodologies: formal-equivalence and dynamic-equivalence.

   In formal-equivalence translations, translators attempt to translate each word in the original language into an equivalent English word. These translations are generally considered more "literal."

In dynamic-equivalence translations, translators attempt to translate the message/meaning of the original-language texts into an equivalent English word or expression. These translations are generally less literal on a word-for-word basis but still seek to capture the meaning of the original-language texts.

2. Discoveries of older manuscripts have affected different versions of the Bible.

The Masoretic Text, written in the 10th and 11th centuries was one of the first discovered and shaped much of the early translations of Scripture. The discoveries of the Dead Sea Scrolls in 1947 revealed some even older manuscripts and shaped translations from that time on. The principle for translators has been the older text (verified) takes precedence over newer texts.

Keeping in mind these two principles, what are the different versions out there and what are the strengths of each one? Here is an overview from Mardel Christian and Education that can assist you in making your choices.[62]

Word for Word Translations

Amplified Bible
Reading Grade Level: 11
Word-for-word plus additional amplification of word meanings.
A popular translation used to understand the meaning of Greek and Hebrew words. Published in 1964 (updated in 1987).

English Standard Version
Reading Grade Level: 7.4

Word-for-word Bible readers of all ages. One of the fastest growing translations, the ESV balances accuracy with literary excellence and readability. A literal update of the Revised Standard Version. Published in 2001.

---

62 "Bible Translation Guide," https://www.mardel.com/bibletranslationguide

King James Version
Reading Grade Level: 12

Word-for-word. English translation of the Bible published in 1611 under the direction of King James I of England. The translation had a marked influence on English literary style and was generally accepted as the standard English Bible from the mid-17th to the early 20th century.

New American Standard Bible
Reading Grade Level: 11

Word-for-word A highly respected, formal translation of the Bible. Purpose of the work was to update the American Standard Version into more current English. Published in 1971. Updated in 1995. The most literal is now more readable.

The Translations that Combine Word for Word and Thought for Thought

New International Version
Reading Grade Level: 7.8

Balance between word-for-word and thought-for-thought. The bestselling translation widely accepted by evangelical Christians. Purpose in translation was to "produce an accurate translation, suitable for public and private reading, teaching, preaching, memorizing, and liturgical use." First published in 1978.

New King James Version
Reading Grade Level: 8

Authors used the original KJV as a benchmark, while working to produce an accurate and modern word- for-word translation Those who want a readable translation of the Bible that is great for study but maintains the poetry of the KJV A modern language update of the original KJV. Purpose was to update and modernize the original KJV but preserve the KJV as much as possible. Published in 1982.

New Living Translation
Reading Grade Level: 6.3

Balance between word-for-word and thought-for-thought based on the work of 90 Bible scholars and a smaller team of English stylists. These scholars and stylists went back to the original languages and sought to produce the closest natural equivalent of the message in natural, contemporary English. Published in 1996.

New Revised Standard Version
Reading Grade Level: 8.1-10.4

Balance between word-for-word and thought-for-thought. A widely accepted translation in the tradition of the King James Version. Purpose was to make a good one better. Published in 1990. A Bible for all Christians.

Thought for Thought or Optimal Equivalence Translations

Contemporary English Version
Reading Grade Level: 5.4

Thought-for-thought.Written at an elementary-school reading level, the CEV is readable and understandable for the modern reader. Published in 1995.

Christian Standard Bible
Reading Grade Level: 7

Optimal Equivalence places equal value on faithfulness to the original text and readability for a modern audience. Bible readers of all ages. A translation that provides an accurate, clear text in contemporary English, suitable for public reading, personal study and sermon preparation.

International Children's Version
Reading Grade Level: 3

Thought-for-thought. *The International Children's Bible®* was the first Bible produced for children in 1982 and even today it is still one of the most easily read and understood versions of the Bible.

Paraphrases

The Message
Reading Grade Level: 5.5-10 depending upon the passage.

Thought-for-thought paraphrase. Put together by Eugene Peterson, this version converts the original languages into the tone and rhythms of modern-day American speech while retaining the idioms and meaning of the original languages. Complete Bible published in 2002.

The Living Bible
Reading Grade Level: 4

The Living Bible is a simplified, easy-to-read rendition of the Bible in effective, contemporary English put together by Kenneth Taylor in 1971.

Some Difficulties Associated with Bible Study

Studying the Bible is not an easy thing for most people. Fifty-eight percent of Americans wish they spent more time reading or listening to the Bible and only sixteen percent of American adults read the Bible daily.[63] Why is this the case and, more importantly, what can we do about it?

1. A lot of people today simply don't like to read. In our culture, we get news and information in different ways. Ours is a digital and visual society in which reading doesn't seem to be stressed as much as it once was. That means that when we ask the people in our group to read and/or study the Bible, that's not something that they are naturally inclined to do. What can we do about it?

   There isn't a shortcut for getting in a person in the Bible and the Bible in a person, but there are tools we

---

63 "Struggling to Read the Bible Consistently? Here are 7 Reasons Why," https://equippinggodlywomen.com/faith/struggling-to-read-the-bible-consistently/

can use. Become aware of the audio versions of the Bible. Many people today find that to be an effective way to approach reading and several different versions of the Bible are available in audio formats. Utilize, too, the Bible apps. The printed book is not as popular as it was. Apps, though, will likely be with us for a while. Familiarize yourself with the various Bible apps and know which ones will appeal to the group you're working with. Also, don't hesitate to use the video tools you have. There are lots of Bible stories and/or texts that have been made into a video format. Whether it is for kids or adults, know what's there. Don't let the excuse "I don't like to read" resonate. Show your people ways to get into the Bible.

2. When people do start to read the Bible, they sometimes find that it's hard to understand or grasp. This is probably the most common reason cited for why people don't read the Bible. How do we address that?

Understanding the Bible is not as difficult as it is often perceived to be. It is not a code book that has to be deciphered. It doesn't require advanced degrees to be comprehended. While it's true that no one ever fully knows or understands all of the Bible, we can get a basic understanding. It's important to know where to begin reading the Bible. It isn't a novel that is to be read from the first page until the last. Some suggest starting at the Gospel of John[64] and others would point to the Gospel of Mark.[65] I'm not sure there is a right answer, but I think having people start by reading one of the gospels is important.

In addition to knowing where to start, there are also some good tools to aid in understanding. *The Story* by Max Lucado and Randy Frazee is a wonderful

---

64 Christina Patterson, "Top 5 Places to Start Reading the Bible," *iBelieve.com*, https://www.ibelieve.com/faith/top-5-places-to-start-reading-the-bible.html

65 "Where Should I Start Reading the Bible?" *NIV Blog*, https://www.thenivbible.com/blog/start-reading-bible/

tool designed to bring a new reader into the biblical world in thirty-one chapters that tell the chronological story of the Bible. This book is not a Bible, nor should it be considered a replacement for one, but it is a wonderful tool to help people understand the narrative, especially the chronology.

3. Sometimes people think they just don't have time to read it. We are a busy culture and our time is often as precious to us as our money. For a lot of people, they are working a job, raising kids, and trying to manage a household. Time for reading and study is just hard to find. What can we do about that?

    There isn't anything we can do about the number of hours in a day or the amount of responsibilities a person may have. Those are issues that are either fixed or beyond our control. However, we can try to develop a system for busy people to create time for reading. Perhaps we can break a book of the Bible down into ten-minute reading sections. We can make those available to those with whom we work. All of us waste at least ten minutes a day. Ten minutes is one additional time scrolling through my social media newsfeed. Ten minutes is reading an article from an online news source. All of us have ten minutes a day that we can reallocate to spend time with God in his word.

Our Christian Education ministry has to place value and emphasis on reading the Bible and addressing the concerns people have. The ones listed above are real, but they are not the only concerns people do and will have. It does not serve us well to dismiss these concerns. Address them and find solutions so that people will find themselves in God's Word.

Summary

In Sunday school long ago, we taught kids to sing "The BIBLE, yes that's the book for me. I stand alone on the Word of God, the BIBLE!"[66] Though it's an old song, the message is still important. Is the BIBLE still what we stand upon?

Questions for Reflection

1. How would you answer the question, "Why does the Bible matter?" How would you describe the Bible's purpose? What impact ought the Bible have in the life of a Christian?

2. Does the inerrancy of Scripture matter? What does it mean that the Bible is "God's Word" and what difference does that make in a Christian's life?

3. Why do you think people need to know the Bible is true and they can depend upon it? What impact, if any, does the authority and dependability of the Bible have on our Christian Education program? Respond to the statement, "People need an objective truth."

4. How does the Bible reveal God, Jesus and right and wrong to us? What does the Bible tell us about God? Jesus? Right and wrong?

5. How does the scripture impact my serving God? How does reading the Bible broaden my awareness of how and where I might serve him?

6. What version of the Bible is your favorite one to read or study? Why?

7. For those who find Bible reading hard, what can we do to help them? How can we demonstrate the importance of Bible reading without appearing to be judgmental?

---

66 https://www.lyrics.com/lyric/2466462/Bible+Songs/The+B-I-B-L-E

Chapter 7

Quality in My Children's Ministry

"Children's ministry may be the most important ministry in the church."[67] This statement might surprise a lot of lead ministers, but there's a lot of truth in it. The children's ministry is one of the first things new families will check out in a church. It's the ministry that often utilizes the most and affects the greatest numbers of individual families. A church that doesn't pay much attention to the needs of children will have precious few children about whom to be concerned. It isn't the intent of this chapter of this book to give a comprehensive overview of how to do an exciting and successful children's ministry. There are lots of good books that discuss that. Our purpose is to discuss some important principles and concepts for those who oversee, lead or volunteer in children's ministry.

Children matter and teaching them is important. Here are five things we all know but might need to think about again.

1. Kids need a strong spiritual foundation. People go through stages of life where they learn in different ways. Children are in the stage of life in which they are open to hearing and receiving the truth. They desire to learn because they are seeking knowledge.

2. Kids need relationships with Christian adults and kids. Relationships are important for adults and for kids. Children's ministry is a wonderful place for this to happen. Kids can meet other kids and form friendships. They can meet caring adults who love them and can mentor them.

3. Kids are the next generation of leaders. This is a truth that is recognized by most churches. We know that

67 Johnny Johnston, *Fuller Youth Institute, Guest Blog,* https://fulleryouthinstitute.org/story/why-childrens-ministry-matters

in children's ministry we are working with the next generation of church leaders, community leaders and world changers. This is exciting and a responsibility.

4. We need to equip parents to raise Godly families. A big, and sometimes overlooked, component of children's ministry is the equipping and encouraging of parents to help grow and teach their children.

5. Children need to know they are loved by God and others. We have the opportunity in children's ministry to provide a safe place for kids and let them know how much they are loved, both by God and by us.

Children's ministry matters. How, then, do we approach it and attempt to create an environment that promotes quality? Let's first begin with understanding the biblical mandate.

What does the Bible say about teaching children?

The Bible places a high value on children. The Israelites took seriously the task of training children and the cultures around them also believed in passing on values and skills to their own offspring. It isn't a surprise then that we find several passages in the Bible that are clear and direct about the importance of teaching the next generation.

Here is a sampling of what the Bible has to say about adults' responsibilities to children.

Deuteronomy 6:6-7

These commandments that I give you today are to be on your hearts. Impress them on your children. Talk about them when you sit at home and when you walk along the road, when you lie down and when you get up.

Matthew 19:14

Jesus said, "Let the little children come to me, and do not hinder them, for the kingdom of heaven belongs to such as these.

Proverbs 22:6

Start children off on the way they should go, and even when they are old they will not turn from it.

Hebrews 12:11

No discipline seems pleasant at the time, but painful. Later on, however, it produces a harvest of righteousness and peace for those who have been trained by it.

Ephesians 6:4

Fathers do not exasperate your children; instead, bring them up in the training and instruction of the Lord.

Psalm 127:3

Children are a heritage from the Lord, offspring a reward from him.

What are the pillars of a purposeful children's ministry?

Children are not "mini-adults," so how we approach them in ministry has to be more than a "scaled-down" version of what we do with people who are older. Though they are not as intellectually or physically mature as older people, kids can understand and process spiritual truth. Robert E. Clark writes, "Children are capable of learning new concepts, but they are often more influenced by attitudes and actions of others than by the concepts they learn."[68]

Understanding that dynamic helps us establish some important pillars that will help ensure that our children's ministry can be successful, purposeful, and meaningful. There are several different groups and children's ministries that have codified their pillars or foundation. All of them have value and are, substantively, a different way of articulating the same truth. For our consideration, I share these four pillars.

---

68   Robert E. Clark, "Elementary-age Children," *Christian Education: Foundations for the Future*, ed. Robert E. Clark, Moody, 1991, p. 236.

Four Pillars of Children's Ministry

1. Jesus Centered — Your children's ministry is not baby-sitting or giving the kids something to do. It is the first opportunity we have to share the good news that Jesus loves you and wants to spend forever with you in heaven. It is fun infused with incredible love, learning and relationships.

2. Child Centered — Your children's ministry is one in which the driving force is what is best for the child. The programming, events, volunteers are all chosen and planned with impacting the child in mind. We want to impress upon our children that God loves them and so do we. As such, our children's ministry is a welcoming, safe place for kids to be.

3. Connection Centered — Your children's ministry is not just about sharing knowledge and stories. It's about building relationships and connecting kids to other kids and to safe, caring adults who love them and model Jesus to them. It is also about connecting children and parents in a life-long adventure of learning about and growing in Jesus.

4. Serving Centered — Your children's ministry is more than just what the kids in your church can get out of it, it is also about what they can give. To that end, your children's ministry is built on a pillar of service. Kids are not too young to serve and recognize their responsibility to others. Your children's ministry gives them initial opportunities to do for others in ways that are age-appropriate and meaningful.

Building your children's ministry on these pillars provides a good foundation for a strong and vibrant ministry. Now, let's look at some important components to be built on these pillars.

Organize Check-in

One of the most important issues for children's ministry leaders and volunteers to tackle is the one of check-in. This applies to every age of child in your ministry. It won't just happen. You will need to set it up if it isn't in place when you arrive.

An easy and effective check-in for children, one that includes identifying who can pick up the child once the service is over, is crucial. In mid-size and larger churches, the reason for this is clear. You have many kids coming whose parents or grandparents your volunteers might not know. There has to be an identification tag or sticker that connects the child with the appropriate adult.

Smaller churches might not think this matters, but in our culture today, it does. Don't shrug this off thinking everyone knows "Miss Lisa" in the nursery, and she knows everyone. We can't afford even one mistake in this area. Go the extra mile to protect children and parents.

Ensuring the safety of the youngest at church is tremendously important. Parents count on it and need to be able to trust that their little ones are in a safe, secure, and appropriate place.

What Does Quality Organizing Teaching Look Like?

"To be effective teachers, workers and parents, we need to understand the people with whom we work."[69] Often in children's ministry, one person will oversee children's teaching and training from birth through elementary school. Some larger churches divide these groups, but generally, birth through elementary school is under the direction of one leader. Clearly, there are many volunteers in children's ministry. No one person can do all the tasks that need to be completed and it is a wise children's minister who has a core group or an inner circle to help him/her make decisions. However, for most churches, the position of children's minister is broad

---

69 Robert E. Clark, "The Ministry is to People," *Christian Education: Foundations for the Future*, ed. Robert E. Clark, Moody, 1991, p. 219.

and is given to one person. For one who is overseeing or managing children's ministry, it is imperative to understand the differences within the scope of that ministry.

Infants to Toddlers

It is hard to imagine teaching infants, but it's important to consider how your ministry views children from birth to the toddler stage. Clearly, there are some important vetting, background check and security issues that are involved in providing care for the littlest of a congregation. The discussion of these particular issues is coming in a later chapter.

Our focus here is on what we are doing to care for them well and what we do to begin teaching. We begin with basic care for infants through toddlers.

Staffing and numbers are important. Make sure you know what your state's guidelines are with respect to adult/child ratios and staff accordingly.

Dan Ketchum, on the *Our Everyday Life* website, shares a comprehensive list that we would be wise to consider. He writes, "The people on your staff are the most important element, but to ensure the safety of the little ones, your checklist must include everything from record-keeping essentials to important safety items."[70] Here are some items you'll need to consider.

- Storage cabinets
- Check-in desk, office chair and computer
- Landline telephone
- Cribs and crib mattresses
- Bassinets and cradles
- Child-sized tables
- Chairs for children and for waiting parents and volunteers
- Storage bins
- Individual cubbies to store each child's parent-provided supplies

70 Dan Ketchum, "Church Nursery Checklist," March 15, 2018, https://oureverydaylife. com/church-nursery-checklist-7908308.html

- Diaper-changing station
- A barrier between toddler and infant spaces if one doesn't exist in the architecture
- Thick, soft rugs or floor mats
- Video security cameras
- A locked maintenance closet or cabinet stocked with disinfectant, non-toxic cleaning supplies, and back-up baby supplies such as diapers, wipes, toiletries and pacifiers
- Hand-washing station/cleaning sink
- Covered trash cans

In addition to these big items, careful attention should be paid to the little things. Sanitation wipes, paper towels, soft soap for handwashing, sanitizer, disposable cups, masking tape or labels to mark whose bag is whose, and, of course, a good selection of age-appropriate toys.

It's also important to make sure that you have first-aid materials available, a fire extinguisher, and a smoke detector. Do all you can to childproof the room, including making any electrical outlet safe for children and checking all furniture, especially donated or homemade, to make sure it is safe. Insist on having good door gates for toddlers. In coordination with your supervisor (lead minister, administrator, or insurance company) write out guidelines for a bathroom and diaper changing policy. Post information for what your volunteers are to do in emergencies, whether it be a fire, tornado, or hostile intruder. Create a policy handbook, either paper or digital, that all of your volunteer staff have and understand.

Now that we've spent some time talking about how we ensure the safety of infants and toddlers, how do we teach them?

Valerie Wilson writes in *Christian Education: Foundations for the Future*, "Those who work with newborns and infants in the church nursery should view their role as service to the Lord."[71] Nursery workers are doing more than just "watching and rocking babies." They are caregivers. Wilson continues,

---

71 Valerie Wilson, "Infants and Preschoolers," *Christian Education: Foundations for the Future*, ed. Robert E. Clark, Moody, 1991, p. 223.

"they have the responsibility of helping the infant form his or her first and most lasting impression of the place called church. Long before he knows anything about what is taught, he will know how he feels."[72]

In addition to loving children and parents, your nursery workers are some of the first to demonstrate Jesus. How they interact with the littlest ones, what songs they sing; and what stories they tell them plant seeds in their lives. Train and equip your nursery workers to sing songs and tell stories. Produce resources for parents and give them to your workers to share. Spending some time thinking about what message our nursery is sending will help sharpen your focus for this age group.

What do you want your nursery workers to know?

1. They are some of the first people a new young family will meet. They need to see their role as that of an ambassador for Jesus and the church.

2. They set the tone for how a new and/or young family will feel about the church.

3. They can be a great place for parents to find and access Christian family resources.

4. They are being entrusted with the most important people in someone else's life. They need to see how important that is.

5. They are the ones who provide a safe and secure place so a family can become a part of the church community.

From Toddler to Pre-Kindergarten

"It's important that each child in a church's ministry be seen as God's special creation."[73] Teaching children from two years old through kindergarten is a challenge, but one that has incomparable rewards.

72 *Ibid.* p. 223.

73 Wilson, Valerie, "Infants and Preschoolers," *Christian Education: Foundations for the Future,* ed. Robert E. Clark, Moody, 1991, p. 231.

This is a time when children are beginning to process and discover. Casual play, singing songs, art projects and circle time are all opportunities to plant seeds and awaken curiosity in the hearts and minds of young seekers. Leaders and volunteers that work in this area of ministry have a big opportunity and responsibility.

What kind of environment ought there be for children this age? Two, three and four-year-old children are growing and developing, but you will still need to pay attention to the physical environment they are in. As is true in every room, their area needs to be child-proofed and appropriate supplies well-stocked (wipes, paper towels, disposable drink cups). They will also need to have a good supply of age-appropriate and learning-friendly toys. They will also need to have written bathroom and accident changing policies in place. It is also important, with regard to staffing, to have at least two people (adults or adult and older teen) in each room. This allows for bathroom trips and aids in supervision and, occasionally, discipline.

With respect to discipline, have a written, "ministry-wide" discipline policy that your volunteers and parents are aware of and understand. This is discussed more, later in this chapter with respect to elementary school kids, but even with this group, make sure your volunteers/teachers and parents know the expectations and approaches. Utilize age-appropriate "time-outs" and removing from a particular activity approaches. Above all, make sure your teachers, volunteers and parents know there is no physical punishment.

Once the room or area is set up, what about teaching? With respect to what we teach them, we've addressed curriculum earlier. This chapter will focus more on how we teach them. Perhaps the best way to address that question is to provide a sample classroom plan. Here's a guideline of what might help your preschool teachers prepare. Utilize this plan and adjust it to fit the situation you are in.

Preschool/Toddler Class Schedule

1) Before Class Starts:

- It is important to have the teacher in the class when the parents bring the children.
- Have a "sponge" activity ready for the kids to do. It might be a coloring page or a simple art project but have them be able to do some simple and engaging seatwork.

2) Opening:

- Have the children come to a particular spot in the area or room. You can have them in a circle if that works for you.
- Pray with them. You might have to teach what prayer is several times and model it for them. You can say a prayer or have the children take turns. Have the children close their eyes, fold their hands, and stay still while others (or you) are praying.

3) Take Attendance:

- Having your teachers know who each week is there is vital for both security and discipleship reasons. Attendance can be taken in a book, computer system or on a sticker chart. This is a great way to get an assistant or young teacher involved.

4) Bridge Activity:

- Show the students' work from the "sponge activity." Talk about the coloring page or project and why it was important. This is a good time to praise the children for their work. Let them know you love them, and God does, too.

5) Music:

- This component makes some volunteers nervous, but it shouldn't. Kids really aren't looking for quality singing as much as they are looking for enthusiastic singing. Additionally, there are many recorded songs devices that will play them. The point is music matters. Use it.

6) Story :

This is the lesson time. Your curriculum may provide this, or you may have to write it for your teacher/volunteer. Encourage them to not just read the material. Some other things they can do include:

- Acting it out
- Having the children provide sound effects as the story is read.
- Use a video (purchased) or create one to share
- Tell the story and have the children guess what happens next
- Tell the story from a particular character's point of view
- Use puppets to tell the story

Encourage your teachers to be as creative as they can be and provide them with creative tools to make this time a powerful and meaningful time on Sunday morning.

7) Activity :

This is the time where your kids can be active again. According to their age and coordination, utilize one or more of these ideas or others each week. You can have them...

- Create an art project
- Make a puzzle
- Draw pictures and/or color

8) Play:

- Once the story and activity are finished, you will want to allow them a time of play. This is supervised and, perhaps, guided play.

9) Final circle/seat time

Before the class ends, have the children seated and looking at books and/or coloring as parents arrive. That will allow your teacher time to interact with parents while the helper monitors a still setting.

This is not the ultimate in classroom plans, but merely a sample. Utilize the concepts to create the one that works best for you and your volunteers in your particular setting.

Elementary School Kids

Elementary-age children come to us with adventurous spirits, abundant energy, varying attention spans and a hunger to understand why things are the way they there are. Those who work in children's ministry have a wonderful and unique opportunity to interact with and direct the course of the kids that come through their doors on Sunday and Wednesday. There can be more fun and learning in this area of ministry than maybe any other. Yet, it comes with its own challenges. Ed Stetzer writes, "I know the importance of children's ministry. I know that most conversions in most churches take place during those critical children's ministry years."[74]

Let's begin by looking at one of the biggest challenges that people perceive to be in this area of ministry: discipline. It's important that we have a consistent and fairly administered discipline policy. This is an area that can vex many teachers of elementary-aged children. There are several children's ministry specific books that go into great detail on classroom management and different ways to approach discipline. For our purpose, let's address some basic principles.

1. Adopt a discipline policy for the whole ministry and each individual class or group and write it down. Make sure that all of your volunteers have it and it wouldn't be a bad idea to give all of the parents in your ministry a handbook explaining the children's ministry (more on that in a subsequent chapter) that includes what the discipline policy is.

74 Ed Stetzer, Foreword to *How to Drive Real Change in Children's Ministry: Leading KidMin*, Pat Cimo and Matt Markis, Moody Publishers, Chicago, July 19, 2016

2. See discipline as bigger than punishment. Punishment is designed to specifically stop a harmful or wrong behavior. A discipline program is one that teaches and equips the young person to make better individual choices.

3. Have reasonable expectations for the age of child with which you are working and have reasonable consequences for falling short.

4. Explain and/or have your volunteer explain the rules and consequences to each group with which they are working. Include not only negative reinforcers for inappropriate behavior but spell out positive reinforcers for desired behavior. Remember, just saying it one time isn't enough. Repeat. Repeat. Repeat.

5. Apply the rules and consequences / rewards consistently.

6. Inform teachers, volunteers and parents that at no time physical punishment will be applied.

7. Be assertive in stepping in to correct or commend.

8. Be honest about when you make a mistake in enforcing and applying the policy and, above all, cultivate a culture of forgiveness, grace and love.

How do we teach this age group? What do we do to make it fun, meaningful and engaging? Here are some principles that you can build classes and groups upon that will enhance your work with this age group.

1. Model a servant's heart — Kids will learn as much or more from what they see than what they hear and read. If following Jesus is about denying ourselves and taking up a cross, then let them see a servant's heart in the ones that lead and direct them. It's a good reminder for leaders and volunteers.

2. Serve with joy at all times — This is easy to say and write, but not so easy to do. However, neither we nor our volunteers should drag our "bad day" into the

class or group. It really is an opportunity to share Jesus every time we meet. We ought to teach each class or group as if it is our last one.

3. Offer many opportunities to do different things — Give kids choices in ways they can serve and do things. Not everyone is charged up about the same things. Adults aren't and neither are kids. While you don't have to offer hundreds of choices, be mindful of varying the opportunities.

4. Don't lose sight of the kids — This seems like another obvious one, but it is easy to get caught up in the program and forget that we are there for the children. If you don't completely finish a lesson but have a great time of sharing with your group of kids, that may be just fine. Remember, they do have a need to know about Jesus, but they also have needs from living at home, school, siblings, friends, peer pressure and a host of other influences. Keep the kids in mind.

5. Don't forget what it was like to be a kid — Some of the best teachers are those who remember what it was like to be in the fourth grade. That doesn't mean you become the kids' "best friend," but it does mean that you get it.

6. Don't be afraid to think outside the box — The leader of the children's ministry will do better if he/she will allow his/her own creative juices to flow. He/she will also do better to allow others to utilize their own creativity. Volunteers should know they can come to you to share creative ideas and will find a receptive audience. Not that every idea is a good one, but every idea deserves a hearing. Build the environment that fosters and nurtures creativity.

7. Build relationships with your kids — This applies to both the leader and the teacher/volunteer. Kids will respond well to people who they know love them and care about them. You have a great opportunity

to mentor and guide the next generation of leaders. Don't just teach a class or lead a group, help shape a leader.

8. Allow kids to minister — A children's ministry that isn't **just** learning or fun but puts into action serving and ministry is a thriving ministry. Creatively design ways for your kids to participate in "doing ministry." This could involve service projects or having older kids help with a younger kids' class or project. Maybe it involves handing out bulletins to adults in worship one week every two months or so. Be creative and let them engage in ministry now, not just prepare them for later.

These principles can help give energy to your elementary school kids. The best advice? Don't be afraid to try things. Failure is not fatal, especially with kids. Pick up the pieces and do it again a different way. For elementary kids, this is a journey of growth and discovery. Enjoy the trip with them.

Summary

Children's ministry is one of the most satisfying and rewarding ministries of the church. Working with kids can be exhilarating. There is no greater joy than seeing a young person get it. To see them understand Jesus' love for them and to hear them express their desire to make him their Savior and Lord never grows old.

Questions for Reflection

1. If you were asked, how would you describe the importance of children's ministry? What difference does it/can it make in the lives of kids, families and in the life of the church as a whole?

2. Regarding the "Four Pillars of Children's Ministry" mentioned in this chapter, how would you describe the importance of each one? How do they, combined, contribute to a solid foundation?

3. Why is an "organized check-in" system so important?

4. After looking at this chapter with respect to infants to toddlers, what is the impression you want parents to come away with regarding your children's ministry?

5. After looking at this chapter with respect to preschool kids, what is the impression you want parents to come away with regarding your children's ministry?

6. After looking at this chapter with respect to elementary kids, what is the impression you want parents to come away with regarding your children's ministry?

7. Why do you think getting kids engaged in ministry and serving matters? What are some ways you might do that?

8. What would you say is the greatest challenge, opportunity and reward that comes from working in children's ministry?

Chapter 8

Quality in My Student Ministry

Youth or student ministry is one of the most exciting, challenging, and misunderstood ministries of the church. There are many thoughtful and well-written books that address the specifics of how to set up, begin and maintain and excellent group. It isn't our purpose to address all of those issues. In this chapter, we'll look at the big picture, principles, oversight and management, of this vital ministry.

There's been a lot written over the last few years about youth ministry and how it operates most effectively. Greg Stier writes, "We live in an age where youth ministry is under fire. There are those pundits who wax eloquent about the demise of youth ministry and pound the pulpit over the need for something different. Some call youth ministry a ploy of the devil to take teenagers out of big church and give them pablum instead. Others say that we just need to integrate teenagers into the overall life of the church, and all will be well. And some call for a purely intergenerational approach that allows the older to disciple the younger. Still others say it's all about children's ministry."[75]

Stier notes three reasons why youth ministry matters.[76]

1. **God has a track record of choosing teens to accomplish great spiritual feats** — Joseph, Timothy, Esther and David are but a few examples.

2. **God receives glory when the** *"foolish things of the world"* **confound the wise** — Stier writes, "1 Corinthians 1:26-29 makes this crystal clear, "Brothers, think of what you were when you were called. Not many of you were wise by human standards; not many

---

75 Greg Stier, "Why Youth Ministry Mattes More Than Ever," June 22, 2016, https://churchleaders.com/youth/youth-leaders-articles/281422-greg-stier-youth-ministry-matters-ever.html

76 Greg Stier, "Why Teenagers? A Case for the Importance of Youth Ministry," https://gregstier.dare2share.org/why-teenagers-a-case-for-the-importance-of-youth-ministry

were influential; not many were of noble birth. But God chose the foolish things of the world to shame the wise; God chose the weak things of the world to shame the strong. He chose the lowly things of this world and the despised things — and the things that are not —to nullify the things that are, so that no one may boast before him." If this passage is not a case for working with teenagers I don't know what is.

3. **It just makes sense** — Teens are moldable and willing to learn. Stier compares them to wet cement that is ready to be poured and shaped.

Biblical Support for Youth Ministry

Young people are important in God's kingdom. The Bible notes the challenges that youth, youth workers and parents face. Youth face an increasingly difficult culture and parents and youth leaders have a daunting task to present Jesus Christ to them and motivate them to live their lives for him.

2 Timothy 2:15

Do your best to present yourself to God as one approved, a worker who does not need to be ashamed and who correctly handles the word of truth."

1 Peter 3:15

"But in your hearts revere Christ as Lord. Always be prepared to give an answer to everyone who asks you to give the reason for the hope that you have. But do this with gentleness and respect."

1 Corinthians 11:1

"Follow my example, as I follow the example of Christ."

Psalm 1:1-3

Blessed is the one who does not walk in step with the wicked or stand in the way that sinners take or sit in the company of mockers, but whose delight is in the law of the Lord, and who meditates on his law day and night. That person is like a tree planted by streams of water, which yields its fruit in season and whose leaf does not wither — whatever they do prospers.

Romans 9:25-26

As he says in Hosea: "I will call them 'my people' who are not my people; and I will call her 'my loved one' who is not my loved one," and, "In the very place where it was said to them, 'You are not my people,' there they will be called 'children of the living God.

The Bible is clear on the importance of training young people and modeling Jesus to them. It's a task parents and youth leaders must take seriously.

Foundation of Student/Youth Ministry

As with children's ministry, student ministry ought to be built on a solid foundation. It's the answer to the question, "on what is your youth ministry based?" Dave Rahn writes in Youth Worker blog, "If we take our kingdom assignment seriously, we realize the change we seek to bring about in young people is of the supernatural variety. Unless we cooperate with the Spirit of God, our best efforts to develop lifelong followers of Jesus will fall short."[77] Having a relationship with Jesus cannot be underestimated. J.B. Cachila writes, "There will never be a relationship in your life that's more important than the one you have with God in Christ."[78]

---

77 Dave Rahn, "Embracing the Foundations: Five Essentials for Transformational Ministry," https://www.youthworker.com/articles/embracing-the-foundations-five-essentials-for-transformational-ministry/

78 J.B. Cachila, "Why your personal relationship with God matters more than any relationship you have," *Christianity Today*, June 27, 2016, https://www.christiantoday.com/article/why-your-personal-relationship-with-god-matters-more-than-any-relationship-you-have/88803.htm

What kind of youth ministry develops life-long followers of Jesus? It's fair to say that there is no one answer to that. There are as many approaches and styles as there are different personalities of youth ministers and workers. There are, though, some principles that ought to be noted.

1. **Prayer** — Every ministry, but especially youth/student ministry, must be bathed in prayer. Pray for the right adult volunteers to be a part of this ministry. Youth leaders need to continually lift up their students and their families. There are so many hurting kids and families. One of the most meaningful ways to minister to them is to continually pray for them. Youth leaders need to also pray that their kids have a relationship with Jesus and grow in him. Prayer is the single most important thing that a youth ministry can be built upon. John writes in 1 John 5:14-15, "This is the confidence we have in approaching God: that if we ask anything according to his will, he hears us. And if we know that he hears us — whatever we ask — we know that we have what we asked of him."

2. **Bible** — If a youth/student ministry is to develop life-change, then it has to have the Bible at its core. Hebrews 4:12 says, "For the Word of God is alive and active. Sharper than any double-edged sword, it penetrates even to dividing soul and spirit, joints and marrow; it judges the thoughts and attitudes of the heart." There is nothing more important in a person's life than knowing God and the Bible is the way God has chosen to make himself known.

3. **Relationships** — A key component of a thriving youth/student ministry is the opportunity to develop and grow meaningful relationships. Seeing students develop a relationship with Jesus is most important. After that, we want to see kids develop quality relationships with other students and caring adults. Paul writes in Romans 12:10, "Be devoted to one another in

love. Honor one another above yourselves." Whether it been in a small group setting, a mission trip, a fun activity or game, we want to see kids develop with each other and youth leaders the traits Paul describes in this passage.

4. **Parental Connection** — This might seem a bit odd for this particular age group, but a student/youth ministry that engages parents well will only see positive outcomes emerge. The student minister who has a good working relationship with the parents of the kids in his/her group is making a difference, not only for kids, but for families. Joshua notes the importance of a family living for God when he says, "But if serving the Lord seems undesirable to you, then choose for yourselves this day whom you will serve, whether the gods your ancestors served beyond the Euphrates, or the gods of the Amorites, in whose land you are living. But as for me and my household, we will serve the Lord." (Joshua 24:15)

5. **Serving Opportunities** — Youth/student ministries that allow their students to actually minister in real ways are developing and maturing their students and preparing them for a life-long walk with Jesus. The opportunities may include mission trips, serving projects in the community volunteering at the church itself and a host of others. Hebrews 6:10 says, "God is not unjust; he will not forget your work and the love you have shown him as you have helped his people and continue to help them." Help your students to see that their walk with the Lord and work for him is a present thing and not something to wait for in the future.

6. **Connection to the Whole Body** — This is important and often gets overlooked. Aaron Earls, writing for Lifeway Research, reports, "Two-thirds (66 percent) of American young adults who attended a Protestant church regularly for at least a year as a teenager say they also dropped out for at least a year between the

ages of 18 and 22."[79] To address this problem, youth/student ministries have to be intentional about bridging the gap between youth/student ministry and what is often called "big church." We'll address that later in this chapter.

7. **Fun** — The student/youth ministry ought to be a place where kids can come and have a good time. Too often church and the Christian faith is labeled "boring," "stiff," or "dry." A relationship with Jesus is nothing like that. An effective student/youth ministry is a real place where adults and teens can relax, enjoy life, be together and laugh. Crazy events or games can enhance your ministry and make it appealing to kids. Students will invite their friends to a youth ministry that's fun and exciting.

Paying attention to these seven pillars will provide a solid foundation for a strong and vibrant student ministry.

Components of a Strong Youth/Student Ministry

Just as no two youth ministers are alike, no two youth ministries are alike either. Youth ministry is a science where the same elements act or react in the same way under same conditions. Youth ministry is about people and they are all different. It is more of an art in which the Holy Spirit works through the unique traits of an individual to share eternal, timeless truths. The artist Vincent Van Gogh once said, "I dream my painting, and then I paint my dream."[80]

Though they might look different in each group, there are some components that help make a student/youth ministry successful.

1. Equipping not just entertaining — While having fun is important, it isn't the main thing in a successful, strong youth ministry. The big idea is to introduce

79 Aaron Earls, "Most Teenagers Drop Out of Church as Young Adults," January 15, 2019, https://lifewayresearch.com/2019/01/15/most-teenagers-drop-out-of-church-as-young-adults/

80 Vincent Van Gogh, *Your Dictionary*, https://quotes.yourdictionary.com/author/vincent-van-gogh/161177

teens to Jesus Christ and to help them grow and develop in their walk with him. One of the key aspects of this is helping students make their relationship with Jesus their own and not one that has been passed on to them.

Additionally, it is important to emphasize discipleship. What does a follower of Jesus do? How can a teen grow as a follower of Jesus? What should the life of a Jesus' follower look like? What are spiritual disciplines and how do I implement them in my life? These are important questions and are addressed in a strong youth ministry.

2. Emphasize Worship — This component is sometimes overlooked. People, however, don't just instinctively know how to worship or why it matters. While children have likely been exposed to it, this is an opportunity to make worship personal and meaningful. What are the different aspects of worship? What does worship look like? How can I worship, not just in church or youth group? All of these questions can be addressed and will help your students begin to own their worship time and make it their own.

This component is critical because, I believe, this is one of the areas in which we can help bridge the gap between the kids who graduate and leave youth groups and don't return to church. If we can teach them why worship matters and have them sense that worship is their own way to honor God, it may help connect them to the larger church when they graduate. This isn't the only thing, but I'm convinced that those who love the Lord and want to worship him will do it, even when they've left youth ministry.

3. Create a caring culture — This is important for all the young people in your youth/student ministry. The young people you encounter in your church may come to you with all kinds of problems and issues. Here is just a short list of stats from the Pew Research

Center that shows what percentage of American teens find these issues to be major or minor struggles among their peers.[81]

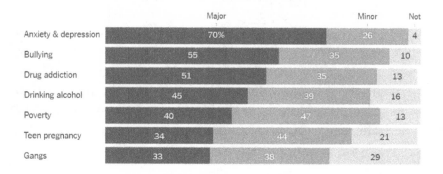

	Major	Minor	Not
Anxiety & depression	70%	26	4
Bullying	55	35	10
Drug addiction	51	35	13
Drinking alcohol	45	39	16
Poverty	40	47	13
Teen pregnancy	34	44	21
Gangs	33	38	29

Pew Research Center

As the graph clearly depicts, kids today are facing all kinds of hard things. They need a safe place where they can find love, care and stability. Youth ministers have to do all they can to be that oasis of security in what is, for many teens, an unsteady and uncertain world.

4. Share leadership — A youth/student ministry that is led by and dominated by just one person can only grow as far as that one person's reach. A wise youth/ student minister will utilize his/her volunteers to share the load. To develop a good flow of creative and fresh ideas, create a team of adult volunteers. To assess how things are going in the group, develop a core group of teen leaders to meet with on a regular basis. Developing other leaders among both adult volunteers and youth will pay dividends for the youth ministry in the present and in the future.

---

81 "What's Going On in This Graph? I Mental Health of Teenagers," *The New York Times*, March 12, 2020, https://www.nytimes.com/2020/03/12/learning/whats-going-on-in-this-graph-mental-health-of-teenagers.html

Aspects that shouldn't be forgotten

Before we wrap up our discussion on youth/student ministry, there are some things that we should address; things that we shouldn't forget.

1. Use Small Groups — The concept of small groups is one that will show up in a discussion of adult education and most understand the principles behind why. We'll look at the benefits of small groups with adults in the next chapter, but for this chapter, why are small groups important for kids?

    A. They provide kids a chance to connect with and interact in a more personal way with a caring adult who may be able to serve as a mentor.

    B. It allows kids another adult in their lives, besides parents and a youth minister, to show interest in them and challenge them to live for Jesus.

    C. Small group leaders can be a positive presence in a teen's life by simply attending games or school events.

    D. Small group leaders can be part of the chain to connect teens to the church as a whole. They are another adult who is happy to see them at church and can work with them side by side in church ministry functions.

    E. Small group leaders can be another safe and trusted adult in a teen's life. Kids can't have too many people that care for them.

    F. Small groups can provide spiritual, moral and emotional accountability to teens who desperately need it.

2. Utilize Games — Utilizing games in youth/student ministry is important. Games can be an important step in team building. It can help students find things in common and get past the initial awkwardness that

can come with meeting new people. Games can be used to break the ice, so students feel comfortable participating in the group.

There are lots of places where you can find good quality games that your kids might enjoy and be helpful to bring your group together. Whatever games you choose, though, there are some important things to consider.

A. Play a variety of games — While it is true that there will be some distinction between the abilities and talent-level of your students, vary the games you play so that natural ability isn't always the major factor for success. Not every game has to be an athletic contest. Not every game has to be a trivia contest either. Use a variety of games that require different skill sets or are simply "luck" based.

B. Play games that don't demean kids — There is nothing wrong with competition and winning or losing. Learning how to manage both is an important skill for young people to develop. There is, though, a difference between a loss and humiliation. Stay away from games that tend to ridicule or mock those who lose. Games are for fun and building up your group. Mocking or ridiculing kids as a result of a game is counter-productive to the overall goal.

C. Play games in which adults can play with teens — This is important, especially when it comes to developing and growing relationships. Having students play games with caring adults is a great way to cultivate an environment of trust, caring and growth. Be intentional about choosing games in which both can play.

D. Play games that are safe and age-appropriate — There may be several games that seem fun but are simply not safe. Don't play games in which the safety or health of your students is jeopardized. Don't play games in which they are to eat weird or unusual things. Don't play games that might cause them potential harm. Don't set up a "slip and slide" on a hill or near a wall. Considering the safety of your students might seem to inhibit the fun you can have with them, but don't neglect it. Water balloon slingshots are fun until someone gets hit and injured.

It's not only important to consider safety with respect to games but consider whether the games you play are age appropriate. Junior high students do not have the same maturity, understanding and self-control as high school students do. Don't set them up for problems by expecting them to play games the way high school students do.

E. Play some games that are specifically designed to build your group — There are many places where you can find team building activities and games. While not every game has to have a specific purpose beyond fun, some of them should. Vary the games you select and purposely choose some of those activities that are designed for building your students.

3. Use Wisdom and Discretion — Be smart and safe in your interaction with students. There will be times when you will need to and want to counsel kids. Don't have a session with you and a student alone. Always have another adult, preferably of the same gender as the student, with you at all times. This is an absolute rule that should never be violated. Doing so puts you and the student at risk. Don't do it. Don't do it. Don't do it.

4. Understand the importance of technology — The use of technology in youth/student ministry is now common. Most youth/student ministers utilize different

methods of tech to communicate with and to enhance the relationship they have with their students. It's important as we continue to dive deeper into the tech pool to get a broad overview of the role tech can play and establish some guidelines for its use.

Here are some ways technology can be effectively used in your youth/student ministry.

A. Bible apps — Introduce your students to different Bible apps for their phones and tablets. Instruct them on how they can best use them. The use of an app for Bible reading is becoming commonplace and the more your students use them and are familiar with them, the more likely it will be that they continue to utilize them.

B. Online classrooms or meeting tools — There are several different ways you can meet with your kids without meeting in the church building or face to face. Investigate Google Chat, Zoom and a host of others that will allow you to meet with a large number of kids. Many of these programs now have a breakout room function which allows you to have small groups meet within the larger group.

C. Podcasts — There are lots of different podcasts available today. Be selective and make your students aware of those that might benefit them. It's also possible for you to do your own podcast and share it with the students.

D. Social media — Many, if not most, of your students will be engaged with social media. Whether it's Facebook, Instagram, Twitter, Pinterest, or a host of others now or the ones yet to be developed, kids are there. Your ministry needs to be where the kids are. Does your ministry have a Facebook page? Do you have an Instagram account? These are important questions that you should be asking. For a ministry to matter, it has to be where the kids are.

E. Messaging Systems — This is important when it comes to communicating with students. The ability to text them is vital. Among students, "90 percent of text messages are read within 3 minutes, and 98 percent are read within 15 minutes."[82] Messaging is an action that will often trigger a response from our students.

F. Use of Videos — The use of video is common practice in many student/youth ministries. YouTube, Vimeo and other sources are frequently utilized by student/youth ministers. It is important to note that there is a lot of quality material on these sites and they can be a tremendous benefit. It's also important to note that the use of this technology requires some oversight. We'll examine those in the next section.

Guidelines for the Use of Technology in Youth/Student Ministry

As is true with many developments of our culture, using technology has many great possibilities and can pose some particular problems. Here are some good guidelines to consider as you work more technology into your ministry.

1. Use good judgment with respect to when you contact students through social media. Don't text or message students at a time when you would not call them at home. It's important to establish acceptable times for you and a student to talk.

2. Implement privacy settings and set up personal boundaries. To do this, you might create a separate page or profile on a social media site for your students

82 Brian Ruhlmann, "Your students are messaging. Are you?" https://www.admithub. com/blog/your-students-are-text-messaging-are-you. October 14, 2016.

to use to contact you. Set up and enforce boundary times when it is appropriate for kids to contact you and the things about which you will talk. Make sure that your students' parents are aware of your social media contact.

3. Adhere to personal standards of holiness. Don't post picture, memes or retweet things that are inappropriate, unchristian or demeaning to others. This not only applies to what is "out there," but be guarded and careful about the personal pictures or statuses you post. Live by the rule that whatever goes out in print on social media is there forever and can be seen by anyone.

4. Communicate how you intend to use video. When you show a video or movie clip to students, make sure that you have previewed it and that you've told your immediate supervisor of your plans. Develop a policy of video use. Do it in connection with your leadership. It doesn't hurt to let parents know your video guidelines. Communicate your policy at the beginning of the year. If you live by the rule "you can't communicate too much," you'll find it an easier journey.

5. Be wise and accountable in all social media interactions. As you would not counsel alone in person, don't video chat alone with a student. If the system you are using doesn't allow for someone else to be nearby, then don't do it. Use texts to convey information, not feelings. It's okay to send words of encouragement or congratulations, but don't initiate a private discussion on a messaging system.

These five guidelines are not the only words on this topic. A wise youth/student minister will work with his/her ministry supervisors or church leaders to develop a system that best fits the situation. The important thing is to have the discussion.

Keeping Students Connected

The final issue for this chapter is addressing the struggle of keeping graduates from the youth/student ministry connected to the "big" church. There are as many answers to this as there are people who work in and volunteer in ministry, but here are some principles that might help set a foundation.

1. Relationships — As appealing as any part of our youth/student ministry might be (and I hope they are all appealing), one of the biggest issues for kids is relationships. What matters are the relationships they build with each other, and the relationships they build with caring adults. Obviously, the greatest relationship we can stress is their walk with Jesus. When students see that ministry (even youth ministry) is deeper than just learning "stuff," it is more likely to be real and important to them. If they graduate with a personal relationship with Jesus and value Christian relationships in general, they will be more likely to seek expressions of it after leaving the youth/student ministry.

2. Develop a heart for serving — If the student/youth ministry has valued serving and has given them opportunities to serve, then they will already know the joy and wonder of serving the Lord. They will not be content to just "let that go." They will seek out opportunities to do that as they've grown. Developing a "heart for serving" in a young person is to develop one for life.

3. Create a hunger for worship — A student/youth ministry that is committed to worship is stressing to the students that worship is real, meaningful and not boring. It is more than singing songs (though that may be part of it). It is more than listening to a message (though that might be a component). Worship is a lifestyle. It is a continual recognition of the presence of

God in our lives. When students are taught to worship, they will crave more.

4. Don't isolate from current adult worship — Do all that you can to make sure your students know that corporate worship is for them, right now. They are not the church of the future. They are a vital part of the church of today. They don't have to wait to be a part of something meaningful. Work with other church leaders to create opportunities for students to see their place in the whole family or community.

These pillars won't ensure that your students will stay engaged, but they will provide a foundation for them to make better individual choices. Don't neglect this issue. We don't want anyone to think they can graduate from their walk with the Lord.

Summary

Youth/student ministry is not easy, but it is important. What we do to love, connect, grow and mature kids in their walk with Jesus can change their lives. Paul wrote to Timothy in 1 Timothy 4:12, "Don't let anyone look down on you because you are young, but set an example for the believers in speech, in conduct, in love, in faith and in purity." That's the goal we have for our kids, too.

Questions for Reflection

1. How would you answer the question, "Why does youth ministry matter?" What difference has it made in your life? How have you seen youth ministry affect others?

2. Throughout the Bible, God has used young people in amazing and incredible ways. What does that tell you about how God views young men and women? How does that impact our view of them and how they might serve?

3. What, in your opinion, are some important aspects of a successful youth ministry? What are some things that cause youth ministries to go "off track?"

4. If you had to identify the greatest need of young people today, what would you say it was and why? How might a youth ministry address that need?

5. Explain why using "wisdom and discretion" is vital when working with students? How will you enforce that in your ministry or any ministry you oversee or work with?

6. What are the advantages and disadvantages of using social media?

7. What steps would you implement to help keep students connected to Jesus Christ after they've graduated? Why is this important? How can "big church" help in this task?

Chapter 9

Quality in Adult Learning

"Adults, as learners are unique, needing an educational approach designed for their own characteristics as learners. Moreover, all adults are not the same."[83] Christian education for adult learners is vital to a growing, thriving church. Perry Downs writes, "Christian Education has a three-fold goal. We teach so that students will think Christianly, act in obedience to the will of God and have hearts that love God and people."[84]

Our approach to adult Christian education has to keep these three principles in mind. We want to motivate, challenge and inspire adult learners to follow Jesus. Lawrence Richards writes, "It's important to recognize parallels between the educational and evangelization ministries of the church."[85] Jesus gave us our mission as he ascended into heaven. He said, "Therefore go and make disciples of all nations, baptizing them in the name of the Father and of the Son and of the Holy Spirit, and teaching them to obey everything I have commanded you. And surely I am with you always, to the very end of the age" (Matthew 28:19-20). That's a verse we know well. Let's examine the Bible's view on learning about Jesus.

Biblical Support for Adult Education

Proverbs 1:5

let the wise listen and add to their learning, and let the discerning get guidance —

---

83 Perry G. Downs, "Adults: An Introduction," *Christian Education: Foundations for the Future*, ed. Robert E. Clark, Moody, 1991, p. 263-264.

84 *Ibid*, p. 269.

85 Richards, *Christian Education: Foundations for the Future* p. 51.

Proverbs 18:15

The heart of the discerning acquires knowledge, for the ears of the wise seek it out.

2 Timothy 3:16-17

All Scripture is God-breathed and is useful for teaching, rebuking, correcting and training in righteousness, so that the servant of God[a] may be thoroughly equipped for every good work.

2 Timothy 2:15

Do your best to present yourself to God as one approved, a worker who does not need to be ashamed and who correctly handles the word of truth.

Colossians 3:16

Let the message of Christ dwell among you richly as you teach and admonish one another with all wisdom through psalms, hymns, and songs from the Spirit, singing to God with gratitude in your hearts.

Psalm 25:4

Show me your ways, Lord, teach me your paths.

Psalm 25:8-9

Good and upright is the Lord; therefore, he instructs sinners in his ways. He guides the humble in what is right and teaches them his way.

The Scripture is clear about the importance of knowing and growing in Jesus Christ. We want to build a stronger, broader foundation than what Sunday morning sermons alone can provide. How do we do that and what are some important principles? Let's take a look.

Four Big Areas of Adult Education

I'm convinced that there are four primary components of a successful adult education program in the local church. A well-rounded vibrant program will consider what learning adults get on Sunday morning; what happens in small groups; what Bible studies are utilized; and how much time and effort does an adult spend in personal Bible study. Let's unpack each of these.

Sunday School

Ed Stucky writes, "Think your church doesn't need adult Sunday school? You could be missing something huge."[86] Stucky argues that attendance in adult Sunday school classes has been on the decline for nearly a quarter century and laments the lack of Bible knowledge among, not only children and students, but adults.[87]

Adults need Bible teaching and training as much as anyone in the church. It is a mistake to assume that someone who is older already knows everything he or she needs to know. Unfortunately, when people get out of school, they believe their days of learning are over. Those of us who believe Christian education matters, especially to adults, have to overcome the preconceived ideas that Sunday school is for children; it's boring and that it is simply unnecessary. What can we do to change these perceptions? Here are some principles that I think can help us build adult Sunday school classes that are vibrant and relevant. Let's take a look.

Principles for Effective Adult Sunday School

1. Biblical — It's important that we recognize this truth again for adults, just as we have for students earlier. If we are going to teach so that people are drawn to Jesus Christ and we aim to see changes in their lives and conduct, we have to teach the Bible.

---

86 Ed Stucky, "How to bring back adult Sunday school (and why you should)," https://disciplr.com/how-to-bring-back-adult-sunday-school

87 Stucky, *Ibid.*

Roberta Hestenes writes, "the Bible was written primarily for adults, to answer adult questions, to deal with adult problems. Finally, then, adult education is vital to the church because it is our opportunity to open the Word of God, the textbook of the church, for people to whom it is ultimately addressed."[88]

If we believe the Bible to be God's inspired word, then we have to be committed to teaching it. Our adults need to know it matters.

2. Relevant — We have to build first on the foundation of the Bible and right after that is the important challenge of showing its relevance. We believe that God's word still resonates for people today. We don't think of it as an archaic book that has little to do with what's going on in the world today.

   Sunday school lessons for adults need to be anchored to God's Word but also firmly connected to the struggles of real people in the real world. Liz Kanoy makes a good point. "The Bible is relevant to all peoples, all cultures, all ages… and it is relevant on its own accord."[89] Relevancy isn't an issue because the Bible struggles to be relevant. It's an issue because we who teach sometimes fail to show the Bible's relevance.

   Our adults should and need to understand that the Bible speaks to them and shows them what God wants them to know about living out their walk with Jesus.

3. Interactive — This is a bit of an unusual component, but important for today's adults. People are not as willing to sit through a lecture. For a lot of people, discussion and engagement matters. A good Sunday

88 Roberta Hestenes, "The Unique Task of Teaching Adults," *Christianity Today*, January 18, 2006, https://www.christianitytoday.com/biblestudies/articles/churchhomeleadership/060118.html

89 Liz Kanoy, "Why You Don't Need to Make the Bible Relevant," December 31, 2018, https://www.crosswalk.com/blogs/christian-trends/why-you-don-t-need-to-make-the-bible-relevant.html

school lesson will incorporate well-written, thoughtful questions that elicit responses. "Getting students to actively participate in class discussions can be a challenge — but one that is worth our time. If we want to guarantee their success, we must get them involved."[90]

What's the key to having good class discussion? Asking meaningful questions. How?

A. Apply the text to yourself first. Think about what it means to you and begin to formulate why it is important in your own walk. This will help you begin to think of what questions you might ask to get your students to apply it to themselves.

B. Plan your questions. Write down several questions that connect the text with your life and with that of your students. You may not use all of these questions in the class discussion or they may serve as a springboard for other questions in the moment but chart some meaningful questions that you know will be good.

C. Ask questions that probe deeper. Don't just ask questions that can be answered "Yes" or "No." A question that begins, "Do you think," is likely to be a surface level question. Questions that focus on "why" things happen or are relevant are more likely to generate thoughtful answers.

D. Allow for questions and answers to lead to other, unplanned, questions. A good discussion will lead somewhere, sometimes to places the teacher did not anticipate. While we have to generally stay on course in the class, don't be afraid to allow a "free flow" of questions. It is an acquired skill to bring the class back after a stimulating discussion and likely the topic of different books, but for

90 Study.com, "How Important is it for Your Students to Participate in Class Discussions?" https://study.com/blog/how-important-is-it-for-your-students-to-participate-in-class-discussions.html

the purpose of valuing discussion a teacher who can allow for a little "free flow" is going to have a meaningful class.

4. Beyond Your Four Walls — This is a concept that we've noted before for other groups, but it matters to adults as well. You want your adult Sunday school class to see that the kingdom of God is bigger than their class or the church they attend. To do that, you will need to interject a missions focus into the class. It would be appropriate for every adult class to have its own mission project it supports. It's also not a bad thing to have your adult classes sponsor projects within the church. Supporting projects should not just be with finances. A healthy, vibrant Sunday school class will have projects that they do to facilitate involvement. Not every class can or will do the same kinds of projects, but every adult class can do something.

   We expect adults already know the value of serving and working, but the truth is we never stop teaching and giving people a chance to get engaged in kingdom work.

5. Fun — This, too, might seem to be a bit strange in a list of meaningful adult Sunday school components, but it's here and not by accident. Like kids and students, adults like to have a good time. While it's true that the fun adults have looks different than the preschool kids, you want your adults to enjoy being in class. How do you do that? Here are some simple suggestions.

   A. Be intentional about building relationships among the people in class. This may involve something as simple as serving coffee and donuts before class or as involved as planning social events for the class to do together. Commit, however, to making sure your class connects.

B. Be genuine as a teacher. If the teacher of the class is real and authentic, then he or she will be seen as a real person and someone with whom the others can connect and have a good time.

C. Laugh. This might seem silly, but it's important. Adults need to laugh. Laugh at the funny things of life. Laugh with each other at the ridiculous and crazy situations of the world. Don't be afraid to laugh at yourselves.

D. Don't take yourself or the class too seriously. This is a bit of a double-edged sword. Adult Sunday school matters and it's important. However, don't take yourself or the class so seriously that it's no longer fun to attend. It's a balancing act between having the right amount of respect for what's going on, but not so intense a mood that it creates harsh discussion, arguments and resentment.

Practical Things to Consider About Adult Sunday School

There are some practical issues that need to be considered as you assess your adult Sunday school classes. Let's take a look at some of them.

Time

One of the first things you'll need to look at is what time your adult Sunday school class will be. Discuss with your church leadership what the most appropriate times might be. If you only have one Sunday worship service, that will likely mean you will offer Sunday school either before or after the worship service. Your adult class will need to be held in connection with the children's and youth classes so the whole family can attend.

If your church has multiple services, then you'll have to decide if you will have class between services or will you offer classes during each of the services. Again, you will want to make sure your adult classes correspond to when you offer children's and youth classes.

Location

Another practical consideration is where to hold adult Sunday school classes. Does your church have an adult education area? Are there available classrooms? Does the area have access to technology? If you have multiple classes, you'll have to make sure you have enough seating and/or tables to accommodate the numbers you may have.

Class location is an important and, sometimes neglected, factor in the success of a given class. It isn't likely that an adult class for parents will do well if their children are in a completely different building. Comfort, proximity to snacks, technology-friendly, close enough to the children's area, and good acoustics are important.

Teacher Qualifications

One of the most challenging aspects in planning adult Sunday school is what requirements do you have for your adult Sunday school class teachers. Clearly you will want someone who is qualified. What does that look like?

1. Mature Christian — Your adult teacher needs to be someone who is a mature Christian who is capable or gifted in teaching and whose walk, to the best of your ability to assess it, is genuine. Ideally, you want them to be life-long learners of the word who want to pass that passion and knowledge on to others.

2. Knowledgeable about what your church believes- It is important that those you have teaching your adult classes are familiar with and understand the basic doctrine of your church. What does your church teach about salvation? How does your church view the inerrancy of Scripture? You will have to make sure your teachers teach in concert with what your church teaches. Nothing will bring more trouble to your adult

classes than to have disputes and controversy of doctrinal issues that are taught.

3. Solid reputation among the believers — You will want to make sure that your teachers are respected among the church body at large. They do not have to be perfect. No one is. However, the quality of their character will need to be visible and spoken of highly.

One of the big issues you may face is whether your church will allow a woman to teach in an adult Sunday school class that has men attending. It is not the purpose of this book to address and resolve that issue. There are many that do so in great detail. For our purposes here, you will need to know and understand the viewpoint of your church and submit to the leadership in how they may decide this.

Length of class

Another important consideration is how long a particular class lasts. Do you want the classes you set up to be continual and just change the topic of discussion every eight to ten weeks or are you better served to offer eight-week classes that have a definite beginning and ending? Do you offer a combination of both types of classes? Permanent classes, those who meet regularly and teach different topics, are important. Short-term class, though, also have a place. Short-term classes are usually topic driven and meet until the topic is completed.

Perhaps the best approach is to offer a blend. Allowing flexibility will allow you to diversify what you offer. Keeping a class going will provide stability and will help develop a culture of establishing relationship. Short-term classes can be a help, too. It's important to keep your teachers fresh. If they can have a break from time to time, it will renew them and keep them wanting to teach.

Groupings

The last of the practical aspects we'll address is the topic of groupings. How do you set up your classes? There are different ways to do it. Let's take a look.

1. Age groups — Sometimes, like with children's and youth classes, adults are grouped by age. There may be a prime timer group for senior saints. There may be another class for 30's-50's and then another class for 20's to 30's. There might be a class for college age adults. Age-based classes tend to be permanent classes.

    There are some benefits to grouping by age. Often people of the same age group have a common experience and life situation. They may have children of about the same age and may have known each other for a long time. However, there are some negatives, too. Common age does not equate to common interest. It's also true that people who are the same age may not be in the same place spiritually.

2. Interest groups — Classes for adults can also be set up around a theme or topic. You may want to offer any adult who wants to come a class on spiritual warfare. Maybe you want to offer a class on prayer. In this setting, what brings the class together is a common interest it the subject matter. These classes would typically be short-term classes.

    There are some benefits to topic driven classes. They can allow a class to go deeper on a particular topic. This type of class also allows for cross-generational relationships to form and develop. However, if the only classes that are offered are short-term, then there isn't a sense of stability and people are less likely to be committed to attending class regularly.

3. Gender grouping — Sometimes you may want to group your adult classes by gender. You might want to

have a men's study or a women's study. These could be permanent or short-term. There are some benefits to this approach. Same gender classes can develop some strong relationships and accountability. They can also deal specifically with particular issues.

While the benefits of gender-specific classes are clear, there are some concerns that ought to be addressed. Gender-specific classes are not always as desirable in the long run. Husbands and wives usually want to attend class together. The content covered in a gender-specific class is not as broad as a general class.

Whatever method you select or combination of methods, communicate it to your leadership team and to the adults in your church. Adult Sunday school classes are important and sometimes neglected. Pray and see if God might not want to use that time to grow your adults.

Small Groups or Life Groups

Many churches today are utilizing small group ministries and it is reinvigorating adult education. Henry Cloud and John Townsend write, "there is no one right way to do small groups."[91] As with other ministries, there are as many different approaches as there are people who try them. The big thing, though, is that if your church is going to make an impact in adult education, you will need to have a plan that utilizes small groups. Ed Stetzer wrote, "If you think community is an important part of healthy church life, and I hope you do, then small groups should also be important to you."[92] Community is a word that we use a lot when describing the church.

Linda Peacore writes, "Talk of community in the church is rooted in various concepts, primary among these is the notion of fellowship or koinonia... The Spirit binds Jesus to

---

91 Dr. Henry Cloud and Dr. John Townsend, *Making Small Groups Work*, Zondervan, (2003). p. 13

92 Ed Stetzer, "4 Reasons Small Groups are Vital to Your Church's Health," March 30, 2015, https://www.christianitytoday.com/edstetzer/2015/march/4-reasons-small-groups-are-vital-to-your-churchs-health.html

the church, the members of the church to each other, and the church to the world."[93]

Small groups or life groups are important to build community in a church body. Let's begin by examining the biblical basis for having a small group ministry.

Biblical Support for Small Groups

The Bible speaks often of the need for the components that are often found in small groups; accountability, fellowship, and caring. Consider these verses.

Hebrews 10:24-25

And let us consider how we may spur one another on toward love and good deeds, not giving up meeting together, as some are in the habit of doing, but encouraging one another — and all the more as you see the Day approaching.

1 Thessalonians 5:11

Therefore encourage one another and build each other up, just as in fact you are doing.

Acts 2:42-47

They devoted themselves to the apostles' teaching and to fellowship, to the breaking of bread and to prayer. Everyone was filled with awe at the many wonders and signs performed by the apostles. All the believers were together and had everything in common. They sold property and possessions to give to anyone who had need. Every day they continued to meet together in the temple courts. They broke bread in their homes and ate together with glad and sincere hearts, praising God and enjoying the favor of all the people. And the Lord added to their number daily those who were being saved.

Proverbs 27:17

As iron sharpens iron, so one person sharpens another.

---

93 Linda Peacore, "What Does it Mean to Say the Church is a Community?" September 29. 2010, https://www.fuller.edu/next-faithful-step/classes/cf565/church-as-community/

John 13:34-35

"A new command I give you: Love one another. As I have loved you, so you must love one another. By this everyone will know that you are my disciples if you love one another."

Benefits of an Effective Small Group Ministry

Why does having a small groups ministry matter? Townsend notes, "small groups provide benefits beyond the scope of their context, topic or materials."[94] What are some of those benefits?

1. Personal Involvement — In the small group setting, participants are far more likely to get involved. Because a small group environment is more open and relaxed, it can invite more engagement among the participants. Personal involvement is not limited to the discussion of a particular topic, but also extends to sharing personally.

2. Smaller Community has a larger appeal — For many churches, getting smaller is huge in trying to reach more people. There's a desire among a lot of people to "do life" with others. They want to share life-stories, encourage and challenge each other. A small community can be an effective way to reach new people. It is less intimidating to attend a small group in someone's home than it is to attend a worship service.

3. Accountability — One of the most important aspects of the small group ministry is the accountability component. Because these groups tend to be smaller, the participants get to know each other. In some groups, accountability is one of the driving factors, but even if that's not the intent of the group, some level of accountability happens when a small group of people meet together regularly.

4. Friendships — One of the most important characteristics of the church is connectedness. We want people to be connected to Jesus and to each other. Small groups

94 Cloud and Townsend, *Ibid.* p. 57.

are one of the best ways to connect people to each other.

Building Blocks of an Effective Small Group Ministry

Now that the benefits and basis for a thriving small group ministry has been discussed, what do you do to build a small group ministry that matters? While there is a lot of good literature on this specific topic, for our purpose, let's consider these four basic building blocks.

1. Pray for direction — As is the case in every ministry, you have to begin with prayer. Ask yourself what is God leading you to begin? What is the Holy Spirit impressing upon your heart? Every ministry launch must be bathed in prayer. Pray for the type of ministry you should have and those who will join you as volunteers.

2. Determine your purpose — Decide what kind of groups or group ministry you are being led to start. There are many different kinds of groups that you could start.

   A. Study Groups — These groups gather for the primary purpose of studying a particular topic or Bible passage.

   B. Discipleship Groups — These groups are for those who want to go deeper in their walk with Jesus. They are for Christians who want to walk more closely to Jesus. Accountability and relationship are key components of these groups.

   C. Life Groups — These groups have elements of both a study group and a discipleship group. They seek to build relationships, with Jesus and with other participants. They also have a study component, too.

   D. Community or Activity Groups — These kinds of groups are not based on study or a "living room" setting. They range from athletic teams to knitting groups.

E. Support Groups — These groups are specifically designed to minister to people in need. They might be support groups for divorce, substance abuse, loss of a loved one or addictions.

3. Determine the details — Regardless of the type of group you start, you'll need to work through some important details.

   A. What will the time frame of the group be? If it is a life group or small group, will it be for a defined period of time? If it is a support group, will it be permanent?

   B. Is it an open or closed group? If it is a life group with a heavy emphasis on accountability, you may want to close it after it begins. If it is a study group, you may want to allow people to join at any time while it is meeting.

   C. Will the groups be home-based or at the church? This is an issue more for groups who have parents with young children. Will there be something for their kids to do while they are in group? Will there be babysitting?

   D. What will the curriculum be? If it is a study-based group, will all groups do the same material, or will you allow each group to select what they want to study?

   E. Will you use technology? Does the group watch a video? If so, do all of your people have the capability to use it? How much of the curriculum do you want to be led by video?

4. Seek and recruit leaders — After spending time in prayer, contact potential group leaders. Once you've

assembled your group, meet with them and share with them your vision for the group ministry.

Now that you have your groups going, it is important to evaluate them and continually work to make them better. One of the most important parts of that is to assess your leaders. What should you want to see in a small group leader? Let's look.

Characteristics of a Good Small Group Leader

1. Spiritually Mature — This is of primary importance. The leaders of your group have to be those who not only can share what matters, but actually live it out. Their Christian character should be known, and they ought to be men or women who are above reproach.

2. Communicates Well — One of the most important traits for a small group leader is the ability to communicate well. This involves sharing information about when the group meets and follow up to encourage group members to stay connected and involved. It's also seen in how s/he is able to share the points of the lesson

3. Able to Facilitate Discussion — This is an important part of small groups (study groups). The ability to ask relevant questions and allow for a free flow of ideas is vital. S/he needs to be able to engage the reluctant and not let those who like to talk dominate.

4. Organized — The group leader needs to be organized. S/he needs to be able to set up or delegate activities or projects the group may want to do. S/he needs to be able to maintain an attendance record and contact those who miss.

5. Ministry Minded — The group leader needs to keep the big picture in mind. S/he is in there to help the group grow and develop. Additionally, s/he is there

to help train others to lead, too. Additionally, the leader has to see that his/her group connects to the church body as a whole. It is not a separate entity.

Developing a small group ministry is important. Jayson Bradley writes, "When you think about it, the New Testament isn't compiled for individuals. It's compiled for the God's people. When it addresses us, it addresses us as an assembly. We need to recognize that we're not intended to serve God in isolation. We need community to thrive.

The small group fills the community role that the typical church is too big to accommodate. With the right leaders, small groups flourish, people mature, and the kingdom grows!"[95]

Personal Study

A final area you will want to think about in adult education is personal study. Encouraging and equipping your adults to study on their own is an important facet that often gets overlooked. If we believe that Jesus Christ can change lives through the Bible, then we need to get the word into our people and our people into the word.

Paul writes to Timothy in his last letter, "Do your best to present yourself to God as one approved, a worker who does not need to be ashamed and who correctly handles the word of truth" (2 Timothy 2:15).

The Hebrew writer observes, "For the Word of God is alive and active. Sharper than any double-edged sword, it penetrates even to dividing soul and spirit, joints and marrow; it judges the thoughts and attitudes of the heart" (Hebrews 4:12).

Teaching adults to study the Bible on their own and developing in them a hunger to do so can be one of the most exciting things we get to do. We sometimes hear this called a "quiet time." These are personal moments that might include Bible reading, meditation, and prayer. Often it is simply

---

95 Jayson D. Bradley, "5 Qualities of a Good Small-Group Leader," Ministry Advice, January 23, 2017, https://ministryadvice.com/small-group-leader-qualities/

spending time alone with the Lord. Here is quick look at the benefits that come from being intentional about these things.

1. **Having a personal quiet time deepens my relationship with Jesus.** If my goal or desire is to be more like Jesus, then spending more time with him only makes sense. My personal walk with Jesus can only grow deeper as I spend time with him.

2. **Having a personal quiet time increases my awareness of how much I need God.** Consistent meeting with him and prayer reminds me of his constant presence. It also reminds me of his constant and consistent provision.

3. **Having a personal quiet time can slow down my hectic, fast-paced life.** It allows me a time to "be still and know that he is God" (Psalm 46:10). It gives me a time for reflection on the things that really matter.

4. **Having a personal quiet time helps me better hear and obey him.** If I am intentionally wanting to hear from the Lord and seeking his direction in the word, I am more likely to find it. Jesus makes it clear, "If you love me, keep my commandments" (John 14:15).

5. **Having a personal quiet time strengthens my ability to live a holy life.** We know that a Christian is called to live differently from the world. Peter writes, "But just as He who called you is holy, so be holy in all you do, for it is written: "Be holy, because I am holy" (1 Peter 1:15-16). A personal quiet time will buoy my resolve to do what Jesus wants me to do.

How do I do that?

We'll begin by looking at what a quality personal quiet time looks like. For our purpose, let's look at a simplified outline for a meaningful quiet time.

1. Set aside a particular time and place to have a quiet time. While it is true that there is no one right place or

time to have a quiet time, having a specific time and place will aid in making it a part of your routine.

2. If you are so led, incorporate music into this time. It is a wonderful way to set a mood and direct your heart and mind.

3. Develop a prayer list and pray each time. Pray for those on your list and pray for understanding both of the Bible text you'll read and how to apply it to your life.

4. Carefully and prayerfully select a book of the Bible to read. You may ask the advice of a Christian friend or mentor if you cannot select one. Commit to read three to five verses each time.

5. Once you've read the text, ask what this is saying and what is going on. Think about what it might mean and how you could apply it.

6. If you have questions, don't hesitate to ask those you know who might have answers.

7. Don't use all of this time for prayer and study. Spend some in quiet reflection. You don't have to have answers or even questions. Just spend some quiet time before the Lord.

Teaching people to utilize these seven steps will help them grow spiritually. We need to note, though, this is not the only system or necessarily the best one. Utilize this outline to create something that works for the people with whom you work. The main thing is to get people to engage in personal study. Dwight L. Moody once said, "In our prayers, we talk to God, in our Bible study, God talks to us, and we had better let God do most of the talking."[96]

Before we leave this topic, it is appropriate that we note the power and importance of prayer. The Bible has a lot to say about what prayer matters.

___

96 Dwight L. Moody, https://www.azquotes.com/quote/662669?ref=bible-study

1 John 5:14-15

This is the confidence we have in approaching God: that if we ask anything according to his will, he hears us. And if we know that he hears us — whatever we ask — we know that we have what we asked of him.

Ephesians 6:18

And pray in the Spirit on all occasions with all kinds of prayers and requests. With this in mind, be alert and always keep on praying for all the Lord's people.

James 5:13

Is anyone among you in trouble? Let them pray. Is anyone happy? Let them sing songs of praise.

Proverbs 15:8

The Lord detests the sacrifice of the wicked, but the prayer of the upright pleases him.

In our Adult Education program, we have to teach and model the importance of prayer. It touches on every aspect of a Christian's life. Philip Yancey describes what might be a good goal for the adults in our ministries to have regarding prayer. He writes, "For me, prayer is not so much me setting out a shopping list of requests for God to consider as it is a way of 'keeping company with God.'"[97] May our ministries develop men and women who are dedicated to being in the presence of the Lord.

Summary

Adult Christian Education is an important part of the church's ministry. Adult Christian Education is an important method of growing in the love and knowledge of God, and the leading of the Holy Spirit. No matter where the adults in our church may be in their Christian journey, Adult Christian Education enhances their development as followers of Jesus.

97   Philip Yancey, "Prayer," https://philipyancey.com/q-and-a-topics/prayer

Questions for Reflection

1. As we consider Adult Christian Education, why do you think it might be overlooked by churches? Why doesn't it get the attention that student or children's ministry might get?

2. As we have looked at Christian Education, we've seen the importance of the Bible and that it is relevant. How can you demonstrate to adults that the Bible is relevant to them?

3. Some churches no longer have adult Sunday school classes. Why do you think that's the case? What do you think about that? How would you relate the importance of an adult Sunday school program?

4. As has been the case in both children's and student ministries, serving matters. Why is that true for adults? How does serving enhance an adult's walk with Jesus?

5. In the discussion of small groups, community was stressed. How do you define community? Why is community important to the body of Christ? What can small groups add to the sense of community for the church?

6. Throughout the discussion of Adult Christian Education, connections were mentioned, both with Jesus and with others. Why is that important to adults? What can we do in the parameters of this ministry to enhance connections?

7. How would you describe the importance of small group leaders? Why do they matter?

8. Adult Christian Education should stress a personal study/growth time. Why does that matter? How do we stress that in the church?

Chapter 10

Bridging with Parents

Glen Schultz writes, "When I became a parent, God gave me the assignment of raising my children as gifts from the Lord. My wife Sharon and I shared the responsibility of training or educating our children according to God's plan."[98] Robert Clark notes, "Biblical education has its foundation in the home."[99]

As Christians, we understand that the building block for God's kingdom is the home. Parents are entrusted with the responsibility of raising and nurturing children in the way they ought to go. The Bible is clear about the role parents have in guiding and training their kids. We who work in the education ministry of the church have a dual responsibility. We are to teach those with whom we have been entrusted and we are to make sure that parents are equipped to do what they are called upon to do.

Biblical Charge for Parental Involvement in Teaching their Children

In a book discussing the nature of Christian Education and to present Jesus is new, fresh ways, it's essential to spend some time examining the role that parents have in this process. The Bible is direct in how it addresses the parent/child relationship. Consider these passages.

Proverbs 22:6

Start children off on the way they should go, and even when they are old they will not turn from it.

---

98 Schultz, *Ibid*, p. 61.

99 Robert E. Clark, "The Church's Allies for Christian Education," *Christian Education: Foundations for the Future*, ed. Robert E. Clark, Moody, 1991 p. 553.

Ephesians 6:1-4

Children obey your parents in the Lord, for this is right. "Honor your father and mother" — which is the first commandment with a promise —"so that it may go well with you and that you may enjoy long life on the earth." Fathers do not exasperate your children; instead, bring them up in the training and instruction of the Lord.

Psalms 127:3-5

Children are a heritage from the Lord, offspring a reward from him. Like arrows in the hands of a warrior are children born in one's youth. Blessed is the man whose quiver is full of them. They will not be put to shame when they contend with their opponents in court.

Proverbs 1:8-9

Listen, my son, to your father's instruction and do not forsake your mother's teaching. They are a garland to grace your head and a chain to adorn your neck.

Deuteronomy 11:18-19

Fix these words of mine in your hearts and minds; tie them as symbols on your hands and bind them on your foreheads. Teach them to your children, talking about them when you sit at home and when you walk along the road, when you lie down and when you get up.

Colossians 3:20-21

Children obey your parents in everything, for this pleases the Lord. Fathers do not embitter your children, or they will become discouraged.

The Bible is clear about the responsibility parents have with respect to their children. James R. Slaughter writes, "We must never confuse the Christian home with a place of residence. The Christian home is not a dwelling place, but a relating fellowship, dynamic and fulfilling. In it we love, serve, talk feel, trust and share our faith."[100]

How Can the Church Partner with Parents?

There are many different ideas and approaches to how this can be accomplished. For our purposes, we'll examine five important steps that can connect a church's educational ministry with the home.

1. **Invite Parents into the Ministry** — This seems like a simple thing, but it is a crucial element if your ministry is to have an impact beyond Sunday or Wednesday. There are many ways this can be done. Every ministry needs volunteers, especially those that work with kids. The parents of the kids in your ministry are an easy resource for you. They can be helpers or staff at your Vacation Bible School. They can host game night or event night. They can bring snacks once a month. The list is only limited by your imagination. Utilizing parents is not limited to children's ministry. Though it may look different for students, parents can still be used as volunteers for events or sponsors for trips. The key is to invite the parents to share in the ministry.

2. **Provide Resources for Parents to use at Home** — For any educational ministry of the church, bridging with parents is a crucial step. Create or develop resources that you can send home with kids or make available online so that parents can know what their children are learning and can reinforce it at home. Do your best to make these resources "user-friendly" so parents will want to use them.

3. **Provide Teaching Time for Parents** — In both children's ministry and student ministry, you can have

100 James, R. Slaughter, "Biblical Perspective for the Family," *Christian Education: Foundations for the Future*, ed. Robert E. Clark, Moody, 1991, p. 566.

an impact on the home and strengthen the bond between you and the parents by offering them training or instructional times. In the student ministry, have someone come and speak about the dangers of social media and how to know when your teen has crossed a line. For the parents of your elementary kids, have someone come and give a talk about safety. Offer a workshop on effective parenting. An effective children's or student ministry will see that the ministry extends beyond the life of the student. See yourself as a minister to the family and your ministry will grow.

4. **Offer some ministry events/opportunities for the whole family** — One of the most important things you can do is expand the programming and opportunities to include whole family times. Whether that is a service or mission project or a fun outing, do some things that are family specific. Try to ensure that the church calendar has events that are "whole family" events. This will prevent the church from becoming too niche specific.

5. **Communicate** — It is important that you communicate with parents. This can be as simple as letting them know a time schedule for regular meeting or as detailed as specifics on a youth trip. If you can utilize social media to create a regular message to parents, that will likely be well received.

Utilizing these five steps will help build a bridge between your ministry and the parents of the kids in your group. Parent support is crucial for the success of your ministry, so don't neglect it.

How the church can help make the family stronger

A positive result of bridging educational ministries to the home is that the church can help make families stronger. The approach here comes more from an adult education perspective and is something that those in charge of adult education ought to consider. Let's take a look.

1. Promote Godly marriages — This seems like an obvious thing, but it matters, especially in the education context. There are many different things for couples to do or attend that can enrich their marriages. Make sure that your church offers at least some of them. There are weekend conferences and getaways; marriage seminars; classes that can be offered at the church; and a host of other things out there. Research them and select what is best for your situation and people. Don't just assume this will take care of itself. It won't. Be proactive. Research and plan this and you won't regret it.

2. Offer groups and/or classes that support broken and blended families — This, too, seems to be obvious. There are lots of people and children who are dealing with broken homes and/or blended families. Plan events that are sensitive to blended and broken families. This is often ignored and makes for some awkward times.

3. Utilize "spiritual parents" for kids whose parents aren't around — You may have kids in your groups whose parents simply aren't there. It may be that dad never comes. It is less likely, but possible, that mom is the one who isn't there. Maybe neither of them show up. Make sure that you show the church is a family by connecting kids whose biological parents are MIA to those who would love them and care for them as "spiritual parents."

4. Provide times for families to connect with each other — It is important, in building strong families, that parents and kids can connect to those around them. Sometimes the beneficial connection is between people of like age and life-station. Sometimes, though, the benefit comes from a cross-generational connection. If you provide the environment for connection, families can and will connect as they are led to do so.

5. Offer encouragement classes — It is wise for a church to offer groups or classes that encourage the family. Maybe what's needed is a group or class for mothers who have preschool children or a class for empty nesters. Assess your group and offer the things that will encourage and challenge them. There are many nationally known groups that offer some of these. Investigate them and see if they might be a fit for your church.

Stress the Things that Matter

One of the most important aspects of bridging your ministry with the families you serve is to emphasize what really matters the most. Glen Schultz writes, "The Bible gives clear direction as to the place God and his Word must have in the home. Christ must be at the center of the home if the home is to be what God intends it to be."[101] If your ministry is to impact beyond the walls of the church building, it will be because we stress two things that really matter. Let's take a look.

1. A relationship with Jesus — Above anything else, we want the people with whom we work to have a relationship with Jesus. We want moms and dads to reflect a walk with Jesus so that their kids see that it is real and not just something we put on for Sunday. This is one of the most important things that we can work on to help the family unit grow.

    Proverbs 3:5-6 says, "Trust in the Lord with all your heart and lean not on your own understanding; in all your ways submit to him, and he will make your paths straight."

    It is good for a family to discuss what it means to "trust in the Lord." How does that look in real life? It is also important, as kids get older, to be able explain to them why things matter. (Exodus 12:26 and Joshua 4:1). A young person whose parents walk with Jesus is

101 Schultz, *Ibid.* p. 109.

more likely to understand what that means and why it is important.

What do we do to help parents/families in this way? Preach and teach a genuine, personal walk with Jesus. Encourage parents to talk to their kids about the things that really matter. Why do we believe what we believe? How does Jesus really impact my life? These are good questions for parents to talk about with their kids.

2. Love unconditionally — We want to foster an environment where the love of God flows into and through the homes to which we minister. A home where mom and dad love unconditionally is a better home for kids to grow up in than one that doesn't. A home where kids are loved unconditionally is a great place for kids to experience, first-hand, how God loves them and begin to internalize that amazing truth.

   That doesn't mean it is a home where anything goes. Proverbs 13:24 says, "Whoever spares the rod hates their children, but the one who loves their children is careful to discipline them." This book is not advocating or criticizing corporal punishment. That topic is addressed in many other places. The key to the verse, for our purpose, is that love and discipline go together.

   How do we help parents in this? Demonstrating this kind of love. If our church is a community that radiates this kind of love, it will be contagious. If we can teach that God loves us this way and it was this love that prompted him to send Jesus, then people might begin to understand it. If they are willing to receive that kind of love, then they are on the road to being able to show that kind of love.

3. Help them understand and model grace — Grace is one of those tough theological issues that we can define in a sense… "God's unmerited favor." However, we wrestle with really trying to grasp and understand

what it means and how it impacts our lives. We know that God, in his grace, provided a way for us to return home to him in heaven. That way is Jesus. We know that we need Jesus because we've sinned. Salvation is God's gift of grace. (Ephesians 2:8-9). We do intellectually get that, but it is hard to really grasp grace.

Hebrews 4:16 talks of our access to his grace. "Let us then approach God's throne of grace with confidence, so that we may receive mercy and find grace to help us in our time of need."

Titus 2:11 reaffirms that it is God's grace that provides salvation. "For the grace of God has appeared that offers salvation to all people."

2 Corinthians 12:9 notes the sufficiency of his grace. "But he said to me, 'My grace is sufficient for you, for my power is made perfect in weakness.' Therefore, I will boast all the more gladly about my weaknesses, so that Christ's power may rest on me."

The Bible talks a lot about God's grace. The word appears over one hundred times in the New Testament. We want to see our ministries and our homes reflect God's grace. We want them to be grace-filled.

How do we help do that? Teach about God's grace. Demonstrate his grace to the best of our abilities. Live in his grace and show his grace by our words and actions. Churches who do that will see that more often in their homes.

4. Equip and encourage them to serve — For young people, something becomes real when it is seen. When kids see their parents living out what they profess, it strengthens their own desire to follow Jesus. The relationship with Jesus moves from being a mind-set or choice into a lifestyle.

James writes in James 1:23-25, "Anyone who listens to the word but does not do what it says is like someone who looks at his face in a mirror and, after looking at himself, goes away and immediately forgets what he looks like. But whoever looks intently into the perfect law that gives freedom and continues in it — not forgetting what they have heard but doing it — they will be blessed in what they do."

How do we help with this? We have to be intentional about providing opportunities for people, especially families, to serve. It is important that families can serve together so that kids see their parents expressing their love for Jesus and others in a real way.

If we stress these things, we will help further the impact our ministries have in the homes of our families. These are the things we want to see happen in the lives of all of our people. If this is what matters the most, we need to do all we can to develop it.

What Parents are Looking for in our Ministries

A survey from 2016 revealed some interesting things about what parents are hoping to find in ministries for the children. Safety is of paramount importance to virtually all parents (96% very + somewhat important). This would likely include their kids being kept safe from physical harm, but many parents may also think of safety in emotional terms. Also noted in this survey was parents' desire for a supportive community for their kids where they have positive friendships with peers who are also exploring faith.[102]

The following chart notes the different areas and expectations.

---

102 *Research Releases in Family & Kids*, "Pastors and Parents Differ on Youth Ministry Goals," March 22, 2017, https://www.barna.com/research/pastors-parents-differ-youth-ministry-goals/

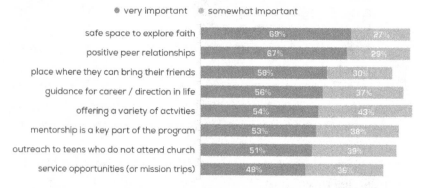

PARENT PRIORITIES FOR THE YOUTH PROGRAM · Barna
% "very" or "somewhat" important among U.S. parents whose teens regularly attend youth group

● very important ● somewhat important

	very important	somewhat important
safe space to explore faith	69%	27%
positive peer relationships	67%	29%
place where they can bring their friends	58%	30%
guidance for career / direction in life	56%	37%
offering a variety of activities	54%	43%
mentorship is a key part of the program	53%	38%
outreach to teens who do not attend church	51%	39%
service opportunities (or mission trips)	48%	36%

February, 2016 | n=296 U.S. parents of teens who regularly attend youth group

While we don't necessarily shape our ministry to fit parents' expectations only, it is important to have an idea of what they are seeking for their kids.

Summary

Bridging ministry and home is important for any Christian education program. As we conclude this chapter, we're reminded of how important it is that there is a partnership between the church and parents. Just a generation after Israel entered the promised land, the people forgot their story.

Judges 2:10-12

After that whole generation had been gathered to their ancestors, another generation grew up who knew neither the Lord nor what he had done for Israel. Then the Israelites did evil in the eyes of the Lord and served the Baals. They forsook the Lord, the God of their ancestors, who had brought them out of Egypt. They followed and worshiped various gods of the peoples around them. They aroused the Lord's anger.

Craig Williford writes, "Many parents fear that their children might grow up and reject their faith, just as the children in the book of Judges did." He continues, "Spiritual formation of children does not require a perfect home, but it does require a home where family members are all working in co-operation with God to assist the growth of each member and the family as a whole."[103]

Those of us in ministry have an opportunity and a two-fold responsibility. What is this opportunity? It is the incredible chance to share with kids and families the most important news that has ever happened. God loves you. Jesus died for you and rose again so you can live forever. We have the opportunity to share that truth.

The responsibility? First, we are accountable to teach the people well. Whether it be children, youth or even adults, we are accountable as teachers. We all need to heed the words of James 3:1, "Not many of you should become teachers, my fellow believers, because you know that we who teach will be judged more strictly."

Second, we are responsible to assist parents in teaching, loving, modeling, sharing and caring for their children. Our ministry is not simply to those who come on Wednesday and Sunday. It is to the entire family. If we take a larger view, it will enrich and expand our ministry outreach.

If we can fulfill this challenge, we'll see stronger homes and more fruitful ministry.

Questions for Reflection

1. Parents are primarily responsible for the spiritual teaching and training of their children. How do we stress that in our ministries? How do we let parents know that we are partners with them?

2. Why do you think many parents abdicate their responsibility to teach and train their kids? Why are so many of them willing to "just let the church do it?" How do we help break that cycle?

3. Inviting parents into ministry was noted in this chapter. Why do you think so many parents avoid this? How can we be more encouraging in this?

103 Craig Williford, "Spiritual Formation in the Home," *Christian Education: Foundations for the Future*, ed. Robert E. Clark, Moody, 1991 p. 584.

4. Providing resources at home was mentioned in this chapter as something important for ministries to do. What kinds of resources do you think parents are most in need of? How can we assess what the parents in our particular church or area need?

5. The chapter also talks about having a training time for parents. What needs do you perceive parents might have that this could help? How could a youth/children's worker get more parents to attend such an event?

6. Serving was mentioned multiple times in this chapter. Why is parents serving with kids so important?

7. Why should the church do all she can to help make families stronger? What are the weaknesses, in our opinion, of families? What can the church do to help them?

8. After reading the section, "Stressing the things that matter," what would you identify as "the things that matter?" Why do you think some of those things are hard for parents to stress with their kids?

Chapter 11

Mastering the Practical

Robert Clark writes, "The church that Jesus Christ is building in this world is still his primary means of reaching the world with his 'good news.' At the same time, people, resources, and programs must be properly organized and coordinated for the church to carry out effectively its educational mission of guiding people to maturity in Jesus Christ."[104]

While we have spent ten chapters examining the spiritual and relational components of educational ministry, there are also some practical issues that need to be addressed.

Budgeting

The first of these is setting a budget. While that is not a glamorous part of ministry necessarily, it is a crucial element. The Bible has a lot to say about stewardship and handling money. Consider these passages.

1 Corinthians 4:2

Now it is required that those who have been given a trust must prove faithful.

Proverbs 3:9

Honor the Lord with your wealth, with the first fruits of all your crops.

Luke 14:28

"Suppose one of you wants to build a tower. Won't you first sit down and estimate the cost to see if you have enough money to complete it?"

---

104 Robert E. Clark, "The Church's Strategies for Christian Education," *Christian Education: Foundations for the Future*, ed. Robert E. Clark, Moody, 1991 p.393.

Matthew 25:21

"His master replied, 'Well done, good and faithful servant! You have been faithful with a few things; I will put you in charge of many things. Come and share your master's happiness!'

The Bible stresses how important it is for Christians to handle money in the right way. If you are going to be in ministry, you will have to deal with a budget. "A church budget is a tool that works to balance finances with ministry. It is the financial road map for your church or ministry."[105]

What are some steps to take in creating a budget for your ministry? Recognize that budgeting is basically an accounting for how your ministry will spend the money allocated to you. Here are some elements that you will likely have in your budget.

1. Program costs — this includes curriculum or teaching materials you plan to use. It would also include supplies, snacks or equipment. Anything that you intend to purchase to use "during the program," ought to be listed and included here.

2. Events — this includes trips you might intend to take, conferences, camps or concerts. If you are working with children, it is going to include Vacation Bible School. It would likely need to address the registration for these events as well as the transportation costs in getting there.

3. Outreach — this will include any costs you will incur as you promote the program to those in the community.

4. Maintenance — this includes the things you need to have on a daily basis to facilitate the ministry. Paper, computer, printer, markers, poster board and a whole list of other miscellaneous items that comprise running a ministry on a regular basis.

105 AGF Financial, "Creating a Budget to Strengthen Your Ministry," https://www.agfinancial.org/blog/creating-a-budget-to-strengthen-your-ministry/

5. Discipleship — this includes money set aside to engage in discipleship, one on one meeting with and sharing with those in your ministry. This may be money for coffee or a soda. It might be money for lunch. It may also involve money to buy a couple of books that both of you read and discuss.

6. Appreciation — this includes money for showing gratitude for your volunteers. If your volunteers are important to your ministry, appreciating them is a part of your financial plan.

Some Important Reminders

Be flexible. Hardly anyone in ministry has access to unlimited amounts of money. You will have to wisely allocate the dollars entrusted to you. It is also true that even if and when you submit a budget, the amount approved for your ministry could be less than you submitted. Understand the nature of what a budget is; a roadmap or plan for how to allocate a resource.

Spend wisely. Especially in the church, a wise steward is one who spends what s/he needs and doesn't just spend a budget to make sure it is gone. Just because a certain amount is budgeted doesn't mean it has to be spent. Most churches do not operate that way. Spend wisely.

Receipts matter. Accountability, especially in the area of money, is crucial to the church. Get receipts anytime you spend church money and make sure there is a system in place to submit those receipts. If there isn't such a system, work with church leadership to create one. Knowing how money is spent is crucial for ministry. Don't neglect it.

Communicate with your volunteers. Make sure that those who volunteer in your ministry have an idea of what can be spent to accomplish a particular goal or put on a certain event. It can be frustrating for a volunteer to spend time working on an idea that, from the start, had no chance because of cost.

Be organized. If you receive a church credit card, make sure to separate it from your own. Don't mix church cash and your cash. Keep financial things in order. If you are collecting fees from kids to go to a certain event, don't leave the collected money in a pile on your desk or just tossed into a drawer. Make sure it is safe and counted. Know exactly how much you have and where it is.

Budgeting is crucial part of ministry and often identifies what we think is important. Jamie Dunlop writes, "To understand what really matters to your church, look past its vision statement, past its website, past its glossy brochures, past what your pastor says your church cares about — and look at your budget."[106]

Background Checks

One of the most important parts of ministry in our current culture is to insist upon background checks for anyone who works in any way with children or students. It hasn't been that long ago when churches didn't conduct background checks. Churches were the safe haven and people who participated in church services, and helped churches fulfill its mission, had a code of conduct. The last twenty years have been a time of change for churches and their legal liability.[107]

Churches have to respond to the cultural changes around them. Stories of church funds being stolen, children abused, and church shootings have, tragically, littered the landscape. What can be done to help turn the tide? One of the most important is background checks.

What are background checks? By definition, a background check is: "The act of reviewing both confidential and public information to investigate a person or entity's history."[108] There are many formats and companies that will perform a background check for your church. What is involved in a background check? Let's take a look.

106 Jamie Dunlop, "What's Your Church's Real Philosophy of Ministry? Ask Your Budget." *Credo*, June 25, 2019, https://credomag.com/2019/06/whats-your-churchs-real-philosophy-of-ministry-ask-your-budget/

107 "3 Reasons to Run Background Checks on All Volunteers," *Smart Church Management*, January 17, 2018, https://smartchurchmanagement.com/background-checks/

108 *Business Dictionary*, http://www.businessdictionary.com/definition/background-check.html

Churches should run the same background check that would apply to a childcare provider. These background checks include:

- Confirmation of the volunteer's identity
- Criminal records
- Sex offender status
- Driving records
- Reference check
- Child abuse/neglect records

Checking these records will give churches a thorough look at any volunteer's past behavior, especially when it comes to vulnerable populations.[109]

Why Background Checks Matter

1. Protect the church — Those who handle the church's money need to be above reproach and men or women of integrity. It might be surprising, but in the first half of 2014, more than $39 billion was stolen in church related financial fraud.[110] Every church ought to conduct a background check on anyone who is handling the church's money.

2. Protect the children — Those who work with kids have to be men and women of exemplary character. While there is no system that can fully guarantee this, the church needs to do all she can to make sure their children are safe.

3. Protect the congregation — It is a tragic reality of the culture today that church shootings and attacks have become more common. Churches have to do all they can to implement safety in their buildings and to make sure they have trained teams ready to deal with

109 "How Do You Run Church Background Checks?" *Criminal Watch Dog*, https://www.criminalwatchdog.com/faq/church-background-checks

110 "18 Shocking Facts About Church Embezzlement," *Share Faith Magazine*, September 18, 2015, https://www.sharefaith.com/blog/2015/09/18-church-embezzlement/

a hostile intruder. What does protecting the congregation have to do with background checks? Churches need to know who is volunteering for them in areas besides working with children or families. A background check, while not foolproof, is a good step in making sure you have an idea who is working in the church.

Background checks are an important tool to ensure the safety of those who are a part of the church. As we administer the programs of the church, it is a crucial, practical matter to prioritize the safety of all who come.

Parent Permission Forms

Working with children and youth is, inevitably, going to involve taking trips. They will likely be going to camps, conferences, amusement parks, college events and a host of others. As you plan these trips, there will be, no doubt, some parents who will go, too. However, it is also likely that there will be young people who attend and don't have a parent present.

When that's the case, permission slips are invaluable. A permission slip ought to have the following information. Free Church Forms is a good place to obtain some templates for these. Their website is found in the footnotes of this chapter.

These forms ought to include...

- Name of the child
- Name of parent or guardian,
- Contact information
- Medical information
- Medical treatment authorization[111]

Once you have obtained all of these parent permission forms, it is wise to keep them in a file, both digitally and physically. While on the trip, make sure that you have the forms with you. Release forms can designate someone on the trip to make medical decisions for the child or children.

---

111 *Free Church Forms*, https://www.freechurchforms.com/consentforms.html

The Church Law and Tax website has some good advice regarding these forms. This is from their website...

While parent release forms cannot avoid liability for injuries to minors, there are other forms that churches should consider. For example, churches should not allow a minor to participate in any church activity (such as camping, boating, swimming, hiking, or sporting events) unless the child's parents or legal guardians sign a form that:

1. Consents to their child participating in the specified activity.

2. Certifies that the child is able to participate in the event (e.g., if the activity involves boating or swimming, the parents or guardians should certify that the child is able to swim).

3. Lists any allergies or medical conditions that may be relevant to a physician in the event of an emergency.

4. Lists any activities that the parents or guardians do not want the child to engage in; and

5. Authorizes a designated individual to make emergency medical decisions for their child in the event that they cannot be reached.

Ideally, the form should be signed by both parents or guardians (if there are two), and the signatures should be notarized. If only one parent or guardian signs, or the signatures are not notarized, the legal effectiveness of the form is diminished. Having persons sign as witnesses to a parent's signature is not as good as a notary's acknowledgment, but it is better than a signature without a witness.[112]

Making sure that parents have signed off on the activities with which their kids are engaged is vital. Don't ignore it.

112 "Parental Permission and Medical Consent Forms," *Church Law and Tax*, https://www.churchlawandtax.com/cltr/2017/november-december/parental-permission-and-medical-consent-forms.html

Summary

Effective management and oversight of the practical issues of budgeting, background checks and parental permission forms will aid in making your ministry as effective as it can be. There are no shortcuts and inattention to any of these components can cripple and even end a ministry. It happens far too often in churches. Don't let it happen in yours.

Questions for Reflection

1. Why is it important for those in ministry to pay attention to the practical details? How does that impact ministry?

2. Respond to the statement, "Your budget demonstrates the things you value in your ministry."

3. Why is how you budget important with respect to how you conduct your ministry?

4. Organization is a key to successfully handling money and receipts. How can you become better organized? Is this a strength or a weakness? What techniques might improve your organizational skills?

5. Explain as you might to a volunteer why they need to have a background check. Suppose you are in a small church where everyone knows everyone. Explain how you would push for volunteers, even in that situation, to have background checks.

6. Describe why parental permission forms matter.

Printed in the USA
CPSIA information can be obtained
at www.ICGtesting.com
LVHW091302131023
760665LV00003B/472